Caroline Palmy stands for lsoul fully expanding into h⋯up and be a light and lead⋯inspiring. Caroline's intuitive ⋯⋯⋯⋯ ⋯⋯ ⋯⋯⋯⋯⋯ ⋯ love, alignment and honoring she feels to Source. This book is the book of a spiritual leader .

- Karin Monster-Peters, energy healer and life purpose coach

Caroline is a truly beautiful soul, who inspires the world with her strong, yet gentle energy. She is a healer who has drawn on her own life experiences and now powerfully shares them with others, guiding each person back to a place where they can live in joy. Healing and reconnecting with your heart is a key step to freedom and happiness.

- Janet Groom Writer & Wordsmith

Caroline is an amazing healer who is open to her own healing path and this expands into what she is able to pass on to others. Caroline has deep knowledge, empathy, compassion and a rich spiritual connection which transcends this lifetime. I am honoured to have travelled with her in this life and in others. Love to you, dear lady.

- Alison Smith, Astrologer

Caroline epitomises everything around love and being loved. You know you're in a good space when you're around her and her healings. She is a wondrous visionary woman.

- Sashka Hanna-Rappl, Author | Speaker | Creator of Brand Your Soul(r)

Despite being deeply grounded in the flow of life - raising three teenage kids as a single mother -, Caroline has the power to turn the prosaic aspects of living into a path of self-discovery, enlightenment and inspiration. She has a talent for inspiring a sense of "energizing calmness" in those who have the opportunity to meet her by touching souls with her gentle and yet powerful insights.

- Stefania Poli, neurofeedback/ biofeedback therapist

I was struggling for years with trying to find a way to move past the hurt and anger of the horrible things my ex-husband did to me. I tried everything but nothing worked until I was blessed to find Caroline. She led me through a series of guided meditations that enabled me to finally find true forgiveness. My life has moved into positive changes since. Caroline has a true gift.

- Angela Brittain, Life Coach

Caroline really knows how to speak to the heart of a person. She is not afraid to lay it all on the table and speak from both the pain and joy of the human experience. Her work is both touching and profound

- Sean Patrick, Managing Director at That Guys House

Caroline is such an amazing beautiful soul, she holds you in love so you can relax and just feel at peace. She has the ability to touch your soul. I am honoured to call her a soul sister.

- Lysa Black, Heart Healer & Mentor

Caroline is one of the most loving and gentle souls I know. Her energy is filled with love and she sees everyone with so much compassion and offers her wisdom so generously. I love how she shares her stories and challenges with such an open heart and by doing so she helps others to feel safe enough to open up their hearts too. I highly recommend working with Caroline and know she will always show up fully and shower her soul sisters with unconditional love.

- Karina Ladet, intuitive, healer, writer & passionate heart-centered entrepreneur.

Caroline is one of those pure, sparkling, wise souls that reaches out and touches you with her bright, engaging mind, refreshing authenticity and wide open heart

A conduit of spiritual inspiration and well-being expertise, it is her true vocation to share her healing gifts for the benefit of others.

As well as being a wonderful mother with a fascinating and courageous story to tell, her expertise combined with her intuitive and caring nature makes Caroline a beloved friend and powerful healing guide to many.

- Maggie Kay, Inspirational Coach and founder of Thrivecraft. Author of Diving for Pearls: The Wise Woman's Guide to Finding Love.

Caroline Palmy is a rare gem of a woman. She has a loving heart with great gifts to offer the world. Caroline enriches peoples lives with her wisdom and presence.

- Lara Waldman, Abundance Activator

Dear Alison,

thank you so much for helping me embrace myself for who I truly are.

You are an amazing soul and fellow Leo

Warm hugs

Conversations With ME

How going through a divorce has helped
me reconnect with myself again

with Love
Caroline

CAROLINE PALMY

This edition is published by
That Guy's House in 2018

© Copyright 2018, Caroline Palmy
All rights reserved.

No part of this publication may be reproduced, stored, in a retrieval system, or transmitted, in any form or by any means without permission of the publisher.

A Note from the Publisher:

This book is a memoir. It reflects the author's present recollections of experiences over time. Some names and characteristics have been changed, some events have been compressed, and some dialogue has been recreated.

A Note from the Author:

This is a work of creative non-fiction and memoir. I have tried to recreate events, locales and conversations from my memories of them. In order to maintain their anonymity in some instances I have changed the names of individuals and places, I may have changed some identifying characteristics and details such as physical properties, occupations and places of residence. Furthermore, some parts of this book have been fictionalised to protect individuals and do not accurately represent events.

www.ThatGuysHouse.com

HEY,

Welcome to this wonderful book brought to you by That Guy's House Publishing.

At That Guy's House we believe in real and raw wellness books that inspire the reader from a place of authenticity and honesty.

This book has been carefully crafted by both the author and publisher with the intention that it will bring you a glimmer of hope, a rush of inspiration and sensation of inner peace.

It is our hope that you thoroughly enjoy this book and pass it onto friends who may also be in need of a glimpse into their own magnificence.

Have a wonderful day.

Love,

Sean Patrick

That Guy.

To my three amazing, most wonderful, and courageous children

M, M, & S

I am so very proud of you.

I love you.

FOREWORD

Caroline Palmy is one of my absolute favorite people in the spiritual community.

We met in 2014 at Doreen Virtue's Angel Tarot Reading and Angel Therapy courses in Zurich. Back then, she was learning how to better help others in their lives by using angelic guidance and working with the angels to deliver messages of hope and support to her clients.

I didn't know at the time that this mission was also personal. I didn't know that she was going through a difficult separation and divorce.

You see, Caroline has always had such a serene, peaceful, soothing energy. When I talk with her, I immediately go into a place where I feel calm and supported.

Caroline has always been a Mom (with a capital M) first and foremost. Everything else came after her kids. I was always in awe of the way she was able to keep her priorities straight, especially in a day and age when the Internet has kind of taken over most of our free time and the rigors of the working life can take so much time and energy that the kids get a lot less than they should.

This book, Caroline's memoir, details her journey to honor herself and her children while dealing with her ex during their separation and divorce. She handled his power games and supported her children with the calm grace I know her for.

Divorce is never easy, especially when your spouse moves on quickly. It is even harder when your ex treats your children with indifference. Add in a stepmother who treats the kids with disdain and like competition, and you have what Caroline has been facing for the past 10 or so years.

But Caroline made it a point to be there for her kids, to make it easier for them, to stand in for them when her ex was careless and to step up for them when he was plain old rude and irresponsible. She soothed and calmed them when he made it seem like his stepchildren were more important to him by giving them more of his time and attention.

During the last 10 years, Caroline has worked to better herself and the world. She felt that sharing her stories would help others deal with their own. She's learned a lot and generously shared what she's learned with her friends and her followers on social media. Her work highlights and uses the lessons she's faced.

They say life can either make you bitter or make you better, and Caroline's story is one of getting better not because you have to, but because you choose to. She's faced her tendency to be a people-pleaser and, instead of letting herself fall into victim mode, being a doormat, or resentfully giving up, she used her experiences to show that she could be strong, independent, and empowered. She didn't shrivel up and take everything her ex threw at her. She took a deep breath (or two) and made a point to be strong for herself and for her children.

As I said, Caroline handled her separation with grace and in the flow of love. She made a point to allow her ex a chance to be there for her children, she examined herself and her motivations and actions during their marriage and afterward, and she helped her children (and herself) grow as a result of the trials they faced.

If you are a parent who is empathetic and sensitive who is facing a divorce or separation from an uninvolved, seemingly uncaring partner, this book will give you some insight about how you can find yourself again, stand your ground, and how to use the experience to know yourself better and to be an advocate for yourself and your children.

Even though I am not separating from my spouse, I've found inspiration in Caroline's story. Her courage in facing her ex and his new partner – and also making her children her absolute #1 priority is inspiring. I've loved watching her grow as a human being, sharing her lessons and the wisdom she has gained from them.

I hope you enjoy reading Caroline's memoirs as much as I have.

With kind respect,

Sue Ellis-Saller

CONTENTS

Foreword xi

Contents xv

Introduction 1

Always Wanted to Live On My Own 5

Hardest Part.. 13

The Flat 19

Being Judged... 25

Simplicity Less Is More 31

Or Forever.. 37

Just Put the Blame on Me 43

Discoveries at The Spa 51

Catherine Homesick 59

First Weekend Without Kids 65

He Just Knows the Right Things To Say 71

Lost in the Living Room... 77

Snake Bite.. 85

Guilt 93

You'd Better Behave.. 99

I Can't Accept the New Situation 105

Four Girls Against Horatio 111
Taxes 119
Chips on The Floor 125
Summer Break 131
Horatio Doesn't Want to Go 137
It Is Her Loss... 145
He Always Cooks Well 151
Dad's Kind of Christmas Lunch... 159
I'll Pay You Only When We Are Divorced 165
Three Girls at Toy Store 173
Passport Renewals... 179
Twenty Percent Less 187
Vanished Christmas Presents 193
Epilogue 199
A final Wisdom from within:... 203
Acknowledgment 205
Special thanks go to... 207
About The Author 209

INTRODUCTION

Dear Reader,

Welcome to my book and to my life.

These are my memoirs, the stories of what I went through. I share them from my perspective and as I remember them. It is not my intention to get into a blame game; however, some of the stories are raw and I am sharing from my heart. It often felt like I bared my soul while writing these stories; I so clearly remember the feelings I had at the time. I hope you will enjoy reading them and get a sense of where I come from and what my children and I went through.

I've written to the best of my memory. I've also used some of my own words retelling the stories my children have shared with me.

Thank you for your understanding.

My intention is for you to feel inspired by my stories. Hopefully, you might giggle or even laugh or shake your head in sheer disbelief because some of what happened with us is so unbelievable. Yes, real life can sometimes be just as funny as a slapstick story. Humor is the best medicine to get through troubled times.

I share my real-life stories from my heart to yours. I know my children and I grew so much through all of this, and each story I've written was a stepping stone on my path back to being myself, Caroline.

I hope that the short tools I share at the end of each chapter can be of use to you, too. You can always come back to these exercises and redo them at different points in your journey to see how much you've grown and changed, or to remind yourself of the basics.

My book is an acknowledgment of my three gorgeous children and how far we have all come together.

Even though this book is not a "spiritual" book, per se, I use well-known spiritual terms because I feel that we are all spiritual beings here on earth, and coming back to myself was a very spiritual path for me.

In this book, you will find the stories I shared with my dearest and closest friends as I was going through my separation and divorce, and the questions I asked myself for the last 10 years.

To protect the identities of the main characters, I've changed the names of the people involved.

My first-born son I call Mathew; he was just twelve when my ex and I separated.

I called my daughter Catherine in this book; she was eight at the time.

My younger son was five when we split up. I call him Horatio here in the book.

I've called my ex Toni in this book.

Jane is a woman who lived in our area. We met infrequently for play dates with the kids and she'd even been to dinner parties at our home. She's Toni's girlfriend in the stories and she is now his wife.

And there is me, Caroline. I am *the I* in this book.

I am a Heart Flow Healer, helping my clients open the doors to their hearts so they can get back into the flow of love again. Love is our true essence. Yes, I help many beautiful souls to heal from past toxic relationships: from relationships with their parents, to their business or at work, and even from past romantic partners.

I learned through my own journey how important it is to free yourself fully and heal from past painful experiences, so you can live in the moment and be fully present and ready to experience all the wonders waiting for you.

I also help my clients to come back to their essences; tapping into their own guidance and learning to be true to themselves, stepping up for themselves and being more assertive. I help them learn to walk their paths and truly *lead* their lives. We are all so worthy of healing our pasts. Saying Yes to ourselves and No to others is one step along this journey.

If you are going through or if you went through a divorce, remember you are NOT alone. If you have a friend going through a breakup, let her know that you are there for her, even though you might feel like you can't help her so much. Just meeting for a coffee, lending an open ear, or giving someone a hug is what many of us need when we are facing hard times. It's nice to have soul sisters to cheer us on during our journeys. The knowledge that we have support and that there is light at the end of the tunnel keeps us going, one step at a time.

I hope you enjoy the stories I share in this book. You might find yourself in some of them. If you like them, please recommend this book to your friends and family. I'd love to inspire as many of you as possible.

Warm hugs,

Caroline

ALWAYS WANTED TO LIVE ON MY OWN

Sometimes we feel things are off even if we don't know what is wrong yet. Is that true for you?

Oh yes, so true. I felt that something was amiss long before Toni told me. And as usual, I had to be the one to ask.

December 30th, 2008 was the exact evening when I truly felt something was not right and had not been for some time. Something was going on with my husband; I honestly felt there was something he did not want to tell me. Maybe he got fired from his job, maybe he had an incurable disease… A lot of different possibilities ran through my mind.

That evening, like so many before, Toni opted to work on his computer instead of coming to bed with me. I was usually more tired, especially after being with the kids all day long, so I generally went to bed early. It was Christmas break that night though, and I could sleep in a bit the next morning because I did not have to drive the kids to and from the school. I felt a bit less exhausted, so I wanted to stay up to watch some more TV. He did not want to watch TV with me, though.

So, he fled to his computer and I read in bed.

I pondered what I was feeling, and I realized he had been acting strange for a while. So, the next day, December 31st,

I sent him an email because he was working. I asked him what was going on and whether he was OK.

He wrote back that he felt he had to live on his own. He had never lived alone before and so he felt it was time for him to try living by himself. It had nothing to do with me, he said, and there was no one else on the side. He told me that he thought I was a great mom and that we could talk more about it that evening when he got home.

I sat there reading the email and a million thoughts passed through my mind. On one hand, I was stunned and on the other hand, I felt liberated. I knew that my intuition and my feelings were right, something was definitely wrong with him, but he was not ill or out of work as I had feared. He just wanted to leave.

I was saddened because I put so much time and energy into our relationship. Even though I tried to make it work, he was leaving. How easy for him. He was fleeing, leaving the sinking ship, so to speak.

He came home late that evening, as usual. We watched TV together. He brought goose liver (foie gras), one of my favorites, and we shared a beautiful wine. No matter how nice the treats we shared were, it became clear to me that he had made up his mind. It was less a discussion than him telling me that he was leaving.

There was nothing I could do, or even that I wanted to do. I was sick and tired of trying to please him and trying to be the perfect wife.

I felt worthless, too, though. He was just leaving me without even any kind of spirit of "let's try and get this working." No. He took the easy way out.

He explained that he had lived at his parent's home and then later always lived together with one woman or another, so he had basically never lived on his own, alone in a flat.

He also told me that he visited a friend's flat and liked the way it felt. Mathew's godfather was separated and living in his own apartment. Apparently, Toni was impressed by our friend's bachelor pad and it stirred a deep longing to live on his own, too. He felt it was the right time for him to give the bachelor life a try.

He even told me that he'd read articles on separation, and they said that it is better for the kids when parents split up before they are teenagers. According to the research, Toni rationalized, now would be the perfect time for him to move out, as Mathew would be turning twelve soon. It felt like he was trying to explain away any blame or guilt he might have felt about moving out.

It seemed he had gotten very well prepared for this move without bothering to let me in on his plans.

Somehow, it made sense to me. I knew he was an introvert (or so I thought) and, let's face it; he didn't spend so much time with the kids when he was home, anyway, so I could understand his decision, in a way.

But somehow, all of this did not sit right with me. It felt very selfish of him, like he was trying to smooth things over, to make it sound better somehow. It did not *feel right*. My bullshit sensors were tingling. However, there was nothing I could do at the time and I wasn't really interested in going the extra mile to keep him around.

And really, it was liberating for me in a way. I did not have to tiptoe around him anymore. Sometimes, I had felt like I was walking on eggshells just to keep him happy. It was hard for me to always keep the kids in line when he was home so that no one disturbed him. I made sure they were in bed by the time he came home.

He was not a very caring father, either. He wasn't one who wanted to hug his kids in the evening before they went to bed, watch TV with them, or even play a game when he was home on the weekend. He preferred to have his peace and quiet.

And me, yes – what about me? I went out of my way to make him happy. I knew it was a fool's task. Instead of sharing the responsibility of the kids with him every once in a while, I tried to carry it all on my own. It kind of backfired, though, because he had NO idea how hard parenthood actually was. He never valued my work or my struggles with the children.

Yes, I wanted to be a mom. It was my biggest dream as a teenager, but this was full on. It was 24/7 with no support from anyone.

During our marriage, too, I had my dreams of being a happy family shattered. We never went on outings together. It was always me and the kids. Even on weekends, I needed to keep the children away from him because they were too loud, too wild, too demanding, too everything.

So, sitting there, hearing that Toni was going to move out felt like a shock and liberation at the same time.

You know, I later found out that his experience of living on his own didn't last long, as he had already his new girlfriend in the picture. He moved into his new flat in March and she moved in with him in June.

My intuition had been spot on. There was much more to him wanting to move out than simply a desire to live on his own. That story turned out to be a lie meant to smooth things over.

Did I like it? Not one bit. I felt I was owed honesty, at the very least. However, I learned over the coming months and years that there was not much honesty for me in Toni.

When he left, I was able to enjoy much more freedom in my life. I was happy to spend as much time as needed with my kids in the evenings. I was glad I did not have to have dinner ready at 8 pm sharp for Toni anymore. I could eat with my children earlier and then we would enjoy leisurely evenings together. Once the kids were in bed, I sat down and read the newspaper or a book instead of worrying about what Toni wanted. It was such a calm and peaceful atmosphere at home after Toni left. I could finally do what I wanted without having to wait on him.

It was a peaceful time for me, at least for a while.

What did I learn from this? Early on, I realized that sometimes things need to fall apart in order to make space for new things to grow. I learned that, even though he was moving out, my world could and would go on. I realized that I had a survival gene in me, that somehow, I always made the best out of every situation I found myself in.

I was happy to make the best out of being alone, left behind by my husband. It felt so good that my world did not have to revolve around his wishes any longer. It was such a feeling of freedom and peace. I never realized how hard it had been trying to be a good wife to Toni. I was free at last and I could do things MY way.

Wisdom from within:

If it feels off, it usually is. Trust your own instincts. Don't take things at face value. I know it is wonderful to trust and believe others; however, if something feels wrong, pay attention to it. You know best, and your intuition will try to warn you.

I learned to ask for time if someone wanted an answer straight away. When I felt pressured, I was not sure whether I said yes just because I wanted to be a nice girl. I learned to tell people that I would think about their request or question and come back with an answer later. This helped keep me from giving in and saying yes too easily.

You can always take your time to give an answer, and always make sure that you take time to feel into yourself and your feelings. How does saying yes feel for you? How about no? Breathe and just notice how you feel within your body. Do you feel tense anywhere? Does the answer someone else wants from you feel restrictive or somehow uncomfortable. If you need to say no, then say no. You are safe saying No.

HARDEST PART

What was the hardest part of the separation and getting used to your new life?

What was the hardest part going through my separation, you ask? I don't know. It might sound funny, but soon after Toni left, I felt so much lighter. I felt like a huge burden had been lifted off my shoulders. Yes, I could finally see light and happiness in the future for the children and I. It might sound strange, but in a way, I was relieved he had left despite the turmoil it brought on. I felt at peace. It is like the Damocles Sword swinging above me, torturing me for so long, had finally hit and I could put the worst of the experience behind me.

It was over. My marriage had ended and there was nothing I had to do to try to save it. There was no more walking around on eggshells. Even though I felt rejected and deeply unloved, I honestly felt very good about divorcing Toni. There was this eerie calm in me. Somehow, I reconnected with the strength and resolve within myself I had forgotten was there for such a long while.

The children all handled the divorce differently. Mathew was twelve and didn't really have an issue with his father leaving, and Horatio was five and more of a Mommy's boy. So, the heartbreak my sweet and wonderful Catherine had to go through was the hardest part for me in all of it.

At the very beginning, it was so hard for me to hear and see my little girl cry for her daddy. She had been his Princess. Before the breakup, there was nothing she could do wrong in his eyes and nothing he could do wrong in hers. She even sat on her daddy's lap and stuck her tongue out at me.

Catherine and her dad were close. Looking back, though, I realize that they were probably not *emotionally* close. It was likely more about the fact that the always wanted a daughter, and Catherine felt his pride and felt special because she was his wish incarnate.

When Toni left, the world fell apart for Catherine. She'd always known she had Daddy's love when he was living with us. Now that he was gone, all she had was me. Gone was her hero, her knight in shining armor, her *Daddy*, and he wouldn't be coming back to live with us.

So she cried every single evening. It tore my heart out. Every time she went to bed, she cried inconsolably.

And every time she called her dad and spoke with him over the phone just showed her what she was missing. I still don't know whether those phone calls made things better or worse. Letting her talk to him felt right back then. She needed to hear his voice, to know he was still there for her, that he was still her dad through all of this. But sometimes it felt like it did more harm than good.

One evening, she came running toward me with the phone in her hands, devastated. She heard a woman's voice on the line. Apparently, he had not hung up the call correctly and his phone was still open, so she could hear them talking in the background. I took the phone, hung it up, and put it away.

We went back to her room. I sat on her bed, tucked her in and held her tight. She asked me who the woman was. Even though I had a suspicion about who her dad was talking to in the background, I said I didn't know. It was neither the time nor the place to say something to my little girl about the new woman in her dad's life. She was devastated, and I held her. Her dream of Mommy and Daddy getting together again was falling apart and she might have been scared that she would lose her place in his life as well.

Did Toni even realize what he was doing to her? Sometimes I thought the better question to ask was if he cared. I felt he acted so very selfishly in all of this.

Still, it brought me back to the core of my being. I love my kids and I cared so much about their well-being that it was OK that it all fell to me to mend their broken hearts, to be the glue to hold it all together for them, to be there for them when they needed me, no matter how tired, exhausted, or devastated I felt. They gave me the motivation to keep going, one step at a time. It didn't make things any easier, but it did give me the push to be strong for them.

Indeed, the hardest part in all of this was seeing and feeling, first hand, the devastation our separation and my ex's new relationship brought on my little girl.

Holding her in her pain, just being there for her, witnessing her sorrow and hurt, not being able to help her, not being able to bring Daddy back, not being able to ease her pain

– that was pretty tough for me. I am glad I could muster every ounce of strength I had left in me to be there for her and never utter a bad word about her father, even though I wished the earth would open under his feet and swallow him up. I let her know it was OK for her to miss her dad, while I was inwardly shouting at him for being so utterly uncaring and selfish. His part was done with a couple of nice words on the phone to his daughter. He had no idea what drama unfolded when he hung up.

There was a second time he did not properly hang up and Catherine heard that woman's voice again. To this day, I am still not sure whether he let us hear on purpose or whether the Universe conspired to have us hear this woman in the background. For me, it helped me to realize that there was someone else in Toni's life, probably even before our breakup. My daughter learned the hard way that this was just the beginning of a change in her relationship with her father.

There were so many evenings I sat holding my precious little girl in my arms, comforting her. She was only eight years old at the time. I tried to console her, letting her cry, reassuring her, while I was cursing her father in my mind.

In my head, I told him what an A#Ç he was for doing this to his little girl. In my heart, I could not understand how any decent human being could put a child through all of this. I despised him for putting us all through this and leaving me with all of the broken pieces to put together again. How could he?

Deep down, I knew I had to be strong, strong for all three of my children who I was holding things together for. There was only me now. He wouldn't support the kids or me anymore. He was truly gone. He was happily living his new life while I was desperately trying to help our children work through the divorce and the changes it caused in our lives.

This all brought out the lioness in me who had been dormant for far too long. If you are going to hurt my cubs, you better be very, very careful. ROAR!

I knew deep in my heart that this was the turning point for the relationship between my ex and our daughter. Even though Catherine had been close to her dad prior to the divorce, it was now time to nurture the mother-daughter bond between us, without interference from Toni. And we did.

We became so much closer over time and when she was a teenager, we rode the waves together, treasuring each other with deep respect. Nowadays, I am so very, very proud of the young woman she has become despite having gone through the painful separation with her dad, or maybe because of it. There is a saying I don't much like, but it might apply here: "what doesn't kill you makes you stronger." I prefer to say, "going through life's experiences is what we came to the Earth for, and mastering them is a big leap in personal development." We would not be here without both the fun times and the challenges, so we should be grateful for everything that comes our way.

Wisdom from within:

Gratitude is helpful in all circumstances. Concentrating on the good things in our lives and feeling deeply grateful for the little things helped me to step away from the sorrow or overwhelm the separation and divorce brought.

Keep a gratitude journal. Write down five things you are grateful for each day. It can be something small like the fact that the sun is shining, that you saw a beautiful flower, you had a nice cup of tea in peace and quiet, etc. Don't look too far or too hard for things to be grateful for. Write each one down and breathe into it. Feel the gratitude in your heart and also how it opens your heart. Connect with this feeling throughout each day.

When walking on the journey we call life, it is important we also look at the flowers along our paths. May there be many beautiful flowers along your path.

THE FLAT

Did I feel used by my ex or like I was being played?

Oh yes, I constantly felt manipulated by Toni. Of course, some things I only realized in hindsight; however, there was one situation that never felt right to me and I felt he was just using me from the beginning.

After Toni told me he was going to move out, he said that he would keep living at our shared home, pretending nothing had happened, until he found a flat to move into.

This did not sit well with me. I felt like, "OK, if his decision wasn't really already made or if it would be like, 'oh we have a problem, let's discuss' kind of thing," then this arrangement might work.

However, his decision to leave was already made. He was going to move out and the question was *when,* not *if.*

I was usually very accepting of other people's situations and wishes; this time, though, I was ready to move on. I needed to have clarity and space. I was not ready to play pretend – not at all.

My world had fallen apart - he had torn it apart - and he expected me to keep smiling and keep up a façade for his sake? That was definitely too much to ask.

I sat quietly with my feelings for a while and then I told him that I wanted him to move out immediately!

He was taken aback by my decision. His well laid out plans weren't working out as he expected.

I told him that there were enough furnished apartments in our area to rent so he could stay in one while he looked for something more permanent. I did not want him to be in my bed or bathroom or house or life any longer.

This was clearly not how he had planned for things to go, but he got himself a flat, packed his bags, and moved out pretty quickly.

I needed clarity then, not more pretending, and so did our young children. How could I tell my kids that Daddy was going to move out if he continued to live with us for another couple of months?

How did he expect me to act when I knew he was moving out? Should I just pretend like everything was normal?

He probably could, but me? No. I am not as good an actress, especially not in this game. I felt I had been playing the happily married wife for far too long. That mask had fallen off the minute he told me he was going to leave, and I had a hard time putting it back on again. It was impossible.

It felt good to put my foot down and say, "Hey. You are leaving no matter what, so you better leave now so I can start my new life right away, without delay or playing this role endlessly."

I preferred to rip the bandage off quickly and let the healing start.

What did I learn from this? I learned to trust my own instincts and stand up for myself. It did not feel right for him to stay with us. Imagining him being around just made me sick to my stomach. There was also that nagging feeling of him taking advantage of my kindness.

I was so right about things my instinct and intuition told me. I later learned that he *had already signed a rental agreement* for a flat back in November, well before he told me he was going to move out! The flat wouldn't be ready until March, though, and him using the excuse of having to find a flat was not true – I could sense it.

He had driven Catherine to a birthday party in November and it took him hours to come back home. He told me he got lost and just drove around. That might have been the day he looked at the flat, perhaps with Jane. Now it all made sense. I hadn't believed his story in November. Back then, of course, I had no idea what he had been up to all along.

I wondered if he thought I was so stupid the whole time we were married. Maybe. Maybe not.

This situation, though, was as good a time to really start trusting my intuition and start standing up for myself as any other moment in my life. Better late than never.

It felt so fabulous to make this decision, trusting my instinct and sticking to it. It was so clear to me that he had to move out, that I could not stand him any longer, that I did not want to pretend anymore.

When he moved out, it felt good. I could start a new phase in my life: my new life as a single mom.

Looking back, I feel even better about my decision. Can you imagine how I would have felt had he stayed on till March, playing me, using me? Would he have continued the charade of looking for a flat, even though he actually already had one?

Trusting my instincts and knowing that I can be right was a very new experience for me at the time. It's something I've developed more and more over the years since this incident. I am sure it will come in handy for the rest of my life.

If you feel something is not right, trust that feeling. It is your intuition speaking to you. I kind of learned the hard way, but I now know how powerfully my intuition works for me.

Wisdom from within:

Our intuition speaks with us always. We might have forgotten to listen to it though.

Intuition is always very fast – often faster than our thoughts. It is always loving and always expansive.

We might hear an inner voice, see a picture with our inner eye, simply know or sense it in our body.

Trusting our intuition, our first instinct is essential. Sometimes we over analyze or try to rationalize something away, or fear gets the better of us.

Putting my hands on my heart, breathing deeply, and asking my heart what the right thing to do is what helps me.

I alternate the questions. Sometimes I ask, "What would love do?" or I ask, "What would Caroline need now?" (Insert your name when you do this exercise.)

Don't be too hard on yourself if you forget to listen to your intuition. I used to beat myself up over not trusting my gut. We all learn from our mistakes.

Every time you tell yourself, "Oh I knew better," is another time you learn what your intuition was telling you and in what form the message came to you. Be gentle with yourself, always. We are all here to learn this game of life.

♥

BEING JUDGED

Were you ever afraid of sharing the fact that you were splitting up?

Oh yes, I was afraid of sharing my situation with others. I feared what people would think of me. I had no problem sharing the news with my closest friends because I needed their reassurance. With some of my friends, I felt like a problem shared was a problem halved. It took me about eight weeks to share the news with my mom, however, because I was so afraid of being judged by her.

You know, it seemed like my mom was proud of Toni. "Oh, he works in an office. He earns so much money. He is well-educated…" etc. It's funny how her perception of him changed during our marriage. When I met Toni, she was all against him and did not talk to me for weeks. She so wanted me to stay with the boyfriend I was already with at the time. Things changed!

I still remember her telling me how lucky I was because Toni gave me jewelry. In the same breath, she moaned about how my father never got her any jewelry. Obviously, jewelry was the language of love and appreciation for my mom. I remember a time, many years before Toni and I split up when she told me how lucky I was to be with a husband who gave me jewels and I remember how unloved I felt, despite whatever gifts I was given. I wanted to scream at her and tell her, "*Life is not all about jewelry!*" I wanted to tell her that nice jewelry was pretty much all I got from my husband. I felt so emotionally disconnected from him and so alone in the marriage. Yes, I had three wonderful children, but I had no support, unless you count something nice to put around my neck as support. Yes, you can feel lonely even when you are married and also when you are given gifts that seem nice to someone who is outside of the relationship.

My mother made the comment about the gifts I received from Toni and many other comments about her managing while bringing three kids up with no support, which did not really instill a nurturing and trusting feeling in me. So, my mom was the last person I wanted to talk to about my break up, about my failure.

And yes, I felt like a failure. Obviously, I must have done something wrong for him to leave me. I did not try hard enough or do enough to keep things together.

I could just hear her asking me, "What did you do to make him want to leave?" I felt like I was being judged by my mother and by society. I know it always takes two to either make or destroy a relationship, but I felt like I was the *one* to blame.

I know now that breaking up and getting over it goes in phases, just like processing grief.

So, because I had her voice in my head saying good things about Toni, I did not want to contact her at all. I did not want to have to talk to her. I felt very uncomfortable with the thought of sharing the break-up with her, my mother, the woman who seemingly adored my husband, who didn't fully understand who he was on the inside. She only knew the smiling face he put on for everyone outside of our home.

I felt that my mom would want to put the blame on someone because there would be no more fabulous son-in-law showering her daughter with jewels.

However, to my utmost surprise, when I did finally open up and tell her, she was very compassionate and stood by my side. Later, when she started to talk bad about Toni, I had to rein her in, especially when the children were around.

To this day, she is still mad at Toni and Jane, who she has met on occasions at my house. She wonders how this woman could have taken away the father of three kids. The easy answer is because he wanted to leave; he was ready to go.

While I allow my mom to have the hate she feels and maybe the guilt as well, I know deep down that everything happens for a reason. We are all meant to go through our experiences. Toni was meant to leave us, be it for Jane or for someone else. I was unable to leave the marriage myself, despite the fact that I was deeply unhappy. I would not have had the strength to leave, so the Universe made him leave so my children and I could be free and I could learn to reconnect with myself.

What did I learn from this exchange? I learned that it is OK to be open and share what you feel are your mistakes and burdens – especially with family – and that mothers usually side with their children, no matter what. Also, I learned not to fear the judgment of others and to never assume they would judge in the first place. I learned that I feared being judged because I judged myself.

Once I was over it, the world was over it too. A break up is not a blame game. It always takes two to make or break a marriage. You can always look for ways to improve your relationship; however, you should also allow yourself to see the bad parts of your relationship and your partner (or ex-partner). The fault doesn't lie solely with you.

It was not only me that caused our marriage to fail and it was not all his fault, either. It never is just one side. Sometimes you just have to accept the situation, as it is, embrace the lessons, and move on.

I learned not to fight against the breakup, at least not for long. I looked at my situation and learned to take one tiny step forward at a time and to keep going and going. There was really no other option for me. I could have thrown myself to the floor and had a temper tantrum; I could have cried for days or been mad at the situation. Deep down, however, I knew there was nothing I could do to change things and that acceptance was the only way through it. There was a light at the end of the tunnel and I just had to keep putting one foot in front of the other to get to it.

One of my friends told me that, when she heard about the break-up, she thought: "There is nothing coming your way you can't handle." This helped me trust in myself, realizing that I would eventually find my way through the situation and that the experience was a part of my life's journey and nothing more.

Wisdom from within:

I love the serenity prayer. It has helped me in many situations:

God/Universe grant me the serenity

to accept the things I cannot change;

courage to change the things I can;

and wisdom to know the difference.

You can speak this prayer out loud or read it like a mantra, over and over, whenever you need to.

♥

SIMPLICITY LESS IS MORE

Did you ever miss the comfort of being married?

Of course, there were things that I missed about being married. I missed being on the same side as my ex-husband, towing the same line. I missed caring for our kids together, without them being caught in the middle. I also missed the support for my decisions, or for going on vacations with the kids.

When we were together, I remember Toni being happy for me to take the children on holiday, myself. He stayed home and had his peace and quiet and I loved to go do things with the children, like playing at the beach or skiing. It was so much easier when I was alone with the children – much less intimidating than when he accompanied us. When he came with us, he always wanted to stay in the most luxurious hotels, which weren't necessarily the most kid-friendly. I was always so on edge, trying to get my kids to behave properly at dinner, that I couldn't really enjoy the luxuries staying in such a hotel might include.

When I was alone with my kids, it was so much easier for me. We could just act like ourselves. We stayed at comfortable locations that had plenty of options for kids and we could enjoy ourselves with ease.

I always made reservations at our skiing hotel, which was generally the one trip Toni joined us for, a year in advance, as they were fully booked months before our holiday came. When Toni moved out and money got tight, I suggested I could go to a different, less expensive, hotel with the kids. He, of course, was pleased and I was, too. The thought of staying at a stiff hotel was not what I needed at the time.

The kids and I went to a lovely ski lodge close by our home and the hotel was comfortable. In the evening, when we went to dinner and saw the coloring sets with crayons and paper, I nearly cried with relief, it felt so good. The kids and I had a wonderful time during our first skiing break after the separation. They could get up during dinner and walk around, we could laugh out loud, and no one turned their noses up at us.

I loved the simplicity of it all, the ease it brought, and the welcoming feel of a hotel that was geared towards children. It was a place where kids were truly welcome. Changing to a more family-oriented hotel for our trip felt good and was a great start to a new era.

In the more exclusive places we chose to accommodate Toni's taste, the attitude was more like, "Children should be seen but not heard," and everyone always seemed to stare at us. I never felt like I could breathe or relax, it was far too stiff.

When Toni booked his personal ski trip and I saw it cost so much more than I ever spent, I was furious. How could he spend so much when money was tight? How could he blow money while I tried to reduce extra costs?

I was always the sensible one. I never overspent, and I was the one to step down again, easing back on little luxuries in order to save a bit of money. I felt like a fool, though, when I saw him splurging.

I realized that I never felt like I was worth spending money on, not for things for me, at least. I learned that I did not feel good enough.

I know I could have gone to the expensive ski resort. I was angry about saving money for him, so he could spend more without any consideration for us.

For me, the point was not about staying in a fancy hotel, though. I, too, loved the comfort staying in a high-end hotel brought and the service that came with it. It was more the duality of it all. While I was being reasonable and maybe denying myself luxury and comfort, he did not seem to have any qualms about spending extravagantly on himself. He spent what he wanted with the attitude that he deserved a life of luxury. I clearly saw how we were on two levels. I was not considered good enough any longer. While Jane got showered with luxury and comfort and splendid service, I carried our suitcases up the stairs into our rooms.

That was a revealing moment, a moment of truth. Yes, I suppose I did miss the luxury in certain parts; however, I didn't miss the stiffness that came with it.

I took a minute to sit and really listen within my own self, asking, "what does my heart say?" I knew, deep down, I was happier at the casual places. I felt more at home and at ease surrounded by happy and carefree kids. It was a better feeling than any luxury could bring.

I knew to embrace simplicity and comfort over stiffness and trying to show off. I felt I was truly coming home to myself again. I knew I preferred play and fun over jewels and flat smiles any day of the week.

Simplicity is more valuable to me than any luxurious thing could ever be.

So yes, I sometimes miss the comfort I enjoyed during my married life; however, I feel more at ease and much more home enjoying the simple things of life.

Wisdom from within:

"The only constant in life is change," a friend told me once.

Unfortunately, we often want to cling to the old and what we are used to.

Imagine yourself in a boat, gently floating downstream.

You don't really want to go downstream, though. You want to stay where you are, so you try to hold on to the branches of a tree, but the current carries you away.

You feel how hard it is to hold on. Your arms ache; they feel like they are being pulled out of you.

This is sometimes how it feels to hang onto something you should let go of in your life.

Be gentle with yourself. Allow change. Allow yourself to let go, like the trees let go of the leaves in autumn knowing there will be new leaves come spring, and also knowing if they cling on to the leaves, the tree will die during winter.

Imagine being on your boat again, allowing the flow and the ease it brings. Embrace it like an adventure, eagerly observing your surroundings and knowing your boat is taking you to a wonderful place.

It is OK to let go. We can't hold on to anything that does not want to stay. Let go lovingly and embrace the new things coming your way.

Remember crossing the monkey bars on the playground? You have to let go of one bar in order to reach for the next one. This is a good lesson to learn in life.

♥

OR FOREVER

Did you sometimes feel like you were in the wrong movie?

I had that exact feeling on several occasions when I was going through my divorce; however, there was this one time when I just felt like, "WHAT????" I could only shake my head in wonder about my ex's audacity!

I remember standing in my kitchen shortly after he told me he would move out. Toni was facing me and said:

"Maybe this will only be for half a year or a year!"

I had what felt like 2,000 thoughts per second.

I looked at him, thinking:

What?? What is it you want to tell me? Do you feel like you can just step out for a little while and then come back like nothing happened and expect to move on from where you left off?

Do you really feel like you could move out on us, do this to the kids (I was more worried how this would affect my kids than myself) and then come back like nothing happened?

You want to destroy our kids' happiness and security, just so you can have a taste of freedom? And then, if it pleases you, you leave for good and if not, you feel like you can just come back?

You want to dip your toe in the wide ocean but still keep your space here.

NO WAY!

I took a deep breath, looked him squarely in the eyes, and said,

"Or forever!"

Toni was taken aback. I had never talked back to him before and I was never, ever so determined as I was at that very moment.

Who did he think he was? The children and I were not just puppets in his theater. We're human beings who have feelings. It's not like he could dump us and expect us to be waiting around until he graciously considered coming back.

No. If he decided to leave us, then that was his decision. There had been no discussion about whether he would leave, so there would be no discussion about whether he could come back.

Leave and let us in peace!

At that moment, I stepped up to him. I clearly said, "This is the line, you do NOT dare cross it."

I was the lioness defending her cubs. I was done being the timid wife who danced to her husband's fiddle. If he wanted to leave, *fine*; however, we weren't going to wait around for him. Our lives would move on, too – just like his.

I knew that when he left, we would travel down different roads and we would be different people in six months or a year. We would have grown from this experience, and, if he ever came back, then it would be a brand-new ballgame.

I know he did not realize this. He just wanted to keep all of his options open so that he could come home and keep going as we were used to if the new life he so desperately wanted did not work out.

However, for me, a door to my freedom had been opened when Toni said he was leaving. I knew in my heart that if he walked away, I didn't want to have him back, not in the same way anyway. I could taste freedom and peace and I did not want to keep the door open for him to return.

I had been deeply unhappy for years and I wasn't going to continue to live as I had been, *especially* if he ever wanted to come back. We would need to set new rules and I would be expecting something in return for the love and support I gave. I would want an emotional relationship and to feel cared for and nurtured. Otherwise, I didn't want a relationship with him.

This was a pivotal moment for me, a moment where I realized I had already started a new life. I knew deep down inside of me that I wanted to have the freedom that came with Toni not being in my life as my husband any longer. I could get a sense of the happiness that awaited me out there. Little did I know, at the time, that the path ahead would be more difficult than I had expected.

I learned that a marriage is made of two people and that I, myself, had a say in things. I could decide whether I kept the door open for him or not. I could say whether or not I wanted him back.

Up to that point in time, I just went along with whatever he decided for us all. Yes, of course, we had to move around the world because his job demanded it. I was adaptable. I was flexible. I made the best out of every situation he threw at me.

That was no longer the case, though. I realized that I could decide for myself what I wanted and keeping the option open for him to come back whenever it pleased him was definitely NOT something I wanted, especially because I knew he would expect us to take off from where he left off.

Times of change were upon us.

Sometimes decisions are final. Sometimes you realize in your heart that *this is it; this is the end.*

Yes, him leaving was the best thing for us and it would be forever.

Wisdom from within:

Come back to your heart and listen within.

Surround yourself with roses. They help us to connect to our hearts and are also connected to Mother Mary, our amazing heart healer.

I carry a rose quartz with me at all times; it helps me to connect to self-love.

A rose essence spray is also wonderful because even the smell of roses helps us to open our hearts.

Remember:

It is OK to say NO. No matter how hard it feels, it is very much OK to say No to others.

Learn to say YES to yourself, allow some time, breathe, put your hands on your heart and ask yourself, "What outcome or option would I love?"

Take time to listen within yourself and go with whatever feels right for you.

"When you say yes to others, make sure you are not, in fact, saying no to yourself." (quote by Louise L. Hay) This quote has helped me along wonderfully, as I learned to say yes to myself more and more.

♥

JUST PUT THE BLAME ON ME

Were you ever a willing participant in keeping yourself down?

Oh yes. Like I said a few times before, "it always takes two." I was eager to be blamed for everything that had gone wrong in our marriage as much as he was eager to blame me.

I love the beautiful quote by Eleanor Roosevelt, "No one can make you feel inferior without your consent." This quote became an anchoring point for my transformation during the years I faced our separation and divorce. Whenever I felt that I wasn't good enough or I felt like Toni was blaming me again, I remembered this quote and inquired within myself, asking, "What is it that I am allowing?" This is called *mirror work* and can be very helpful in all situations, also in raising teenagers.

As you have seen in previous chapters, Toni tended to blame others for everything, just so he did not have to feel inadequate or feel anything at all, really.

I remember one situation when we were sitting in an office with two child psychologists who helped Mathew and Catherine process the separation and divorce. At the time, I felt it was necessary for my children to have an independent person to go to and share what was coming up for each of them. So, Toni and I were discussing the children with the therapists and considering how we should handle situations in regards to the children's behavior.

Toni complained about how disrespectful our children were. He even mentioned that I did not bring them up properly, that I was not fulfilling my job as a mom.

There I sat again, wondering why he always put the blame on me for everything and anything.

Luckily, at this stage, I was already aware of this behavior and also, I knew my children well. I knew that they acted up when they did not feel comfortable or when they were stressed. This was especially true for Mathew, who was a sensitive Indigo Child. He sometimes got hyper if he was uncomfortable; it was his natural reaction to the energy around him.

Plus, the stress of having the stepfamily, Jane and her two daughters, living at their dad's did not help.

I understood that my children felt left out and were only looking for a sign that they were still loved by their father. It reminded me so much of myself: all I ever really wanted was to be loved and understood.

Nowadays, of course, I understand that I need to accept and love myself first and foremost. We often want love and acceptance from others, though.

While Toni went on about how our kids were acting up and he complained that, compared to those three brats of mine, Jane's two daughters were so well behaved and showed respect to him.

I realized respect was very important to Toni.

I remembered how one of the teachers at the Montessori School we had our kids attend while living abroad shared her wisdom. She explained that, in this beautiful Montessori environment, each child was shown respect. No one was to step on a child's mat, etc. She told me that, when children are treated with respect, they, in turn, learn to be respectful. So, we treat others like we want to be treated.

I saw, at this moment, what a tyrant Toni was.

He DEMANDED respect from everyone around him without showing any kind of respect for anyone, not even his own children. All he did was complain and talk down to them. He even had the audacity to compare his own children to the children of the new woman in his life. How dare he!?

My children were in a completely different situation than hers were. They were only *visiting* THEIR dad, while the other girls lived there, and had their mom present too. My kids were left alone in the jungle, so to speak, without anyone who seemed to be on their side.

So, this all went through my head in a flash. When he was finished complaining, I sat up straight and told him:

"I've only heard the best from the teachers about my children. They know how to behave. Whenever they are over at someone else's place, they behave well. It seems to me that this is less about the children than the adult who is present".

He looked at me, completely stunned. I had to laugh. He probably felt he could tell me what he thought was wrong and I would jump to fix it, as I had always tried to do before.

Children aren't like computers, where we can fix a bug and then they run properly all the time. Children are human beings who react to situations and energy. Most of the time, when children act up, they are uncomfortable. Like toddlers, even older children can throw a tantrum when they are tired. Is it the fault of the child that his need for a nap was neglected by the adult caring for him?

I remember how good it felt to point out the fault in Toni's reasoning, and also how hilarious it felt to hear his order, "I demand respect".

First, I thought, show respect to your own children. Treat them as human beings, not as trained monkeys. Be with them, get to know them, listen to them without judgment. Honestly, I just wanted him to show that he cared for the kids – that was my hope for him all along.

Deep down, I hoped the child psychologists could talk some sense into him; however, that was not their role. They were there to support the children and they stayed impartial, no matter what.

Sitting there, hearing Toni complain about how misbehaved the children were, I realized again that he was so happy to blame me for everything. "Does he ever take responsibility for his own actions," I wondered?

Do I? I remembered that I was so eager to please him and that I used to take the blame for everything that went wrong. I tried hard to make him happy. Where did I respect myself in all of this?

Back when the kids were younger, they would sometimes be up at 7:30 pm when he came home because bedtimes were running late, and he would complain about the kids not being in bed yet.

When I was not ready to sit down to have dinner with him at 8 pm sharp, he sat waiting in front of his plate till I came, just to make me feel guilty because his dinner had gotten cold while he waited for me.

Somehow, him blaming me for the behavior of Mathew, Catherine, and Horatio at his place was the last straw for me. I was so done with his game. I'd had enough. I told him point blank that if he couldn't handle the kids, it was his problem. I also mentioned that he was never an active parent so no wonder he had no idea about how to deal with his children.

Respect needed to be earned and, in the eyes of the kids and myself, he did not deserve any respect at all.

Indeed, I realized I never respected myself when Toni and I were married. It was a sad and humiliating realization. It was time for me to show myself some respect and embrace myself for who I truly was.

He was not doing his part as a father – never had, and never would. All I could do was accept this fact and make the most out of this clarity.

"Just put the blame on me," was over. I was ready to let him take responsibility for his part in how our children behaved when they were with him, and everything else, really. It was time to free myself from all the blame and guilt.

It felt good knowing that my children were doing well overall, and I was a tiny bit pleased that they gave their dad such a hard time. Yes, I admit it honestly. I got a good giggle out of it.

Well done kids, I am proud of you.

Actually, the kids showed me that I did not have to accept every situation as it was and that I, too, could act up and be a bit naughty and misbehaved, myself. Being a good-girl all of the time is tiring and quite boring as well. "Let's dance," I thought, and dance I did… I learned to dance to my own music.

Wisdom from within:

"How others treat you is their karma; how you react is yours," is a fabulous quote from Wayne W. Dyer.

Whenever emotions bubble up from inside you, take a moment to listen within. Ask yourself questions like:

- What are the emotions telling me?
- Why am I upset?
- Why am I reacting to this?
- What does it relate to?

For example, consider if someone called you stupid.

If you feel a bit stupid, you will get upset. If you do not feel stupid, however, you won't react as negatively to the comment.

Also consider where, in your body, you feel the reaction. Is it in your mind, your heart, or your stomach?

Considering why and where we are triggered by the comments of others is a great way to learn so much about ourselves.

♥

DISCOVERIES AT THE SPA

Were there any eye-opening moments after your separation?

I had many; however, being told that I had been abused without even realizing it was one of the most profound for me.

When Toni started staying in his apartment during the week, he came over to the house to be with the kids every other weekend, so I could enjoy some time skiing. I went out so he could spend the weekend with the kids without us having to pretend to be friendly or be uncomfortable together.

He then fully moved into his flat, taking all the things he wanted with him. We spent time agreeing on what he could take, but then he took other things we hadn't agreed on when he moved, and then he came back and took more.

I was upset that he took advantage of my kindness and I resolved to go to his flat and ask for the things he took without my consent. Even though I wanted to, I never did go and demand my possessions back. I still miss that blue pan he took….

The first weekend Toni took the children to his apartment for visitation was approaching rapidly. Even though I had always wished for some time to have peace and quiet all by myself at home, circumstances made this first weekend different. I think every mom would love a bit of rest and relaxation every now and then, but, when it comes with a separation and honoring your ex's visitation schedule, it takes on a different, more depressing and, ultimately, lonely quality.

I could not handle staying home alone that first weekend. Being in a big house all by myself with no kids to take care of, no noise, somehow made everything seem all the more real. No. I was not ready to face this yet. I accepted an invitation from two of my friends to go to a spa weekend with them so that I didn't have to be alone.

I was so relieved to be able to escape and get away from everything for a bit.

It felt good to have friends who looked after me during this time and supported me in my sorrow and hardship.

We had a great weekend – lounging in the spa and enjoying wonderful dinners together. We laughed and talked about toys for single women and discussed how I could best enjoy my newfound freedom. And of course, the champagne flowed!

I remember the moment when we were sitting in our bathrobes in the spa. I had been considering that I needed to apologize to one of my friends, as I felt that I might have come on to her husband at one point in time. I was feeling so lonely and unloved back then, that I was desperate to know I was attractive and other men might want me. She wasn't mad at me at all. She understood, and we hugged and the air was clear between us.

I shared a painful secret with my friends that day: Toni and I had not had sex since Horatio was conceived six years before. Even before that, we only had sex specifically so I would get pregnant.

I opened up to my friends, admitting that intercourse was never pleasurable with Toni and that I never had an orgasm with him. The lack of pleasure wasn't about me, either, as I had experienced orgasms with other men. My pleasure was just never a consideration in our married sex life, and I was too timid to ask for it.

They looked at me in stunned silence, with big compassionate eyes. They hugged me and then one of them told me, "You have been abused."

I shook my head and laughed, "No... no," I said, "Of course not. He never beat me. He never harmed me physically and was mostly honest with me".

My friend took my hands, looked into my eyes, and lovingly told me that Toni was emotionally abusing me.

I still refused to believe it. It simply could not be. It could not have happened. I would know if I had been abused, wouldn't I?

My two good friends opened my eyes to something I did not even fathom: that my ex emotionally abused me. No wonder I had felt so drained and unworthy. I never, ever felt like I was good enough for him.

Then the memories started coming up, like the time when I was home with my firstborn, juggling motherhood and caring for the house, all in a foreign country with no help.

Toni would come home in the evening and ask me how many books I had read during the day while he was at work. He seemed to think that I was living a life of rest and luxury. Most days, though, I did not even have time to fit in a shower and I was utterly exhausted from getting up multiple times a night with our baby.

Another memory came up of the time he asked me why my hair never looked as good when I did it myself as it did when I came from the hairdresser. As if I was some magical hairstylist, not a mom who had been playing all day with my children.

I thought about the many times he sneered at me for wearing T-shirts and jeans *around our home* – I was not properly dressed in slacks, heels, and wearing a full face of makeup. Should I have been rolling around, playing with the children on the floor in my finest dresses, I wondered.

Then it hit me. I realized that I had been emotionally abused the whole time. There was (and is) nothing wrong with me – sexually or otherwise. It was an epiphany for me.

After that weekend, I read every book I could get my hands on that covered the topic of emotional abuse and relationships.

I eventually learned that I am an Empath, or a deeply sensitive person who feels the emotions of others. Because I could intuitively feel Toni's childhood pain, I instinctively wanted to make Toni feel better. I wanted to heal him.

Because I felt so drained by Toni, I really wondered whether he could be a Narcissist. The way that Toni treated me really made me feel that he was.

Yes, it always takes two to make or break a marriage, but I wanted to help him so much I took everything on: all of the responsibility, all of the criticism, all of the childcare and housekeeping, and trying to dress up for him like a "proper" wife. I wanted to make him comfortable and happy, so I gave up the things that made me comfortable and happy.

Learning about this Narcissist/Empath dynamic and realizing I was not the only one experiencing a relationship like ours helped me a lot on my healing path.

The way Toni acted made me feel he just didn't care – not for me, not for the kids, not for anyone. It seemed to me he only cared about how our family looked from the outside, not how it FELT for those who were in it, like me. From what I read and how I understood it, it seemed he had some narcissistic tendencies.

Stepping out of this unhealthy relationship took time for me. I felt timid. He threw his full wrath at me and it hurt me deeply. It took a while for me to fully walk away and time to learn not to let him intimidate me any longer. I needed to learn not to take on the blame and I had to learn to cut the strings.

I was not his puppet anymore.

What a fabulous eye-opening weekend this was for me. The journey back to myself started and the healing had begun.

Realization is always the first step to healing.

I was not blind anymore – not blind to the abuse, not blind to all the wrong that happened, not blind to my own part in it either. I was taking responsibility for things I could control, like my actions and my happiness, and letting my husband and his opinions and abuses go.

Wisdom from within:

Toxic relationships, especially Empath-Narcissist relationships, are being talked about more openly these days.

Lee Harris has launched an e-course about this topic. He also has some free videos and explanations available.

There are several other teachers and healers on the Internet who have videos and classes about Empath-Narcissist relationships.

You can use these tools to feel what is right for you in your life. Don't be afraid to form your very own definition and opinions about relationship dynamics, too.

I always felt I was too sensitive; I should toughen up. Nowadays, though, I know that being an Empath and highly sensitive are my greatest gifts, as they help me in my healing work with my clients.

Embrace yourself just the way you are.

What helped me was hugging myself daily. Yes, hug yourself! You deserve your hugs. You can switch the arms around (the arm that was on top now goes under the other one). Make a point, too, to embrace all the parts of yourself you do not love yet. Embrace all of you; you are an amazing human being, a beautiful soul and a wonderful person.

♥

CATHERINE HOMESICK

Was there a change of perception during the journey?

Oh yes. There was one precise moment when I learned so much about how my ex treated the kids. Once I noticed a particular pattern Toni was prone to, it became crystal clear. I saw this tendency in him in every interaction he shared with the kids and me. I could not close my eyes to it any longer.

This situation was what triggered the Aha! moment for me:

One weekend, Catherine was very disturbed when she came home from a visit to her father's house. Usually, all three of my children were tired and exhausted when they got dropped off, and they were always really happy to be back home.

Horatio often cried when he was finally back in his safe space, letting go of all the stress that built up during the weekend at his father's house.

Mathew usually just locked himself in his room and wanted peace and quiet after a weekend away. He probably enjoyed the comfort of his room and having his own things around, and also being able to breathe and relax.

Catherine was especially sad when she came home that weekend. She did not say much; I did not want to probe.

When I hugged her goodnight while we were sitting on her bed, she started to cry and the story eventually all came out.

It took her a while to calm down from crying. It was OK. I was used to the readjustment time they needed when they came home. I caressed her and hugged her and just held her. I was happy she could cry it out.

Eventually, she started talking. She said she was homesick while visiting her dad.

I hugged her, and I told her, "Of course, my baby. That is normal. You miss Mom when you are at your dad's and you miss Dad when you are here. That is normal and very much OK."

She nodded and cried some more.

Then she said, "You know, Dad was very angry with me. He told me that if I don't stop crying, he would bring me back home!"

What a weird and wrong reaction towards a little child! How could he? I didn't think this was normal behavior from a father who loves his child! Why didn't he just hug her and tell her it was OK, or at least try to soothe her? Why did he need to make her feel bad and ashamed for feeling homesick?

Now, I understand that he might have felt rejected by his daughter, his Princess, who wasn't happy to visit him. However, the fact that he had zero empathy and no understanding and that he was unable to accept the fact that Catherine was homesick – this was beyond my comprehension.

Then it hit me. *That's the way he had always behaved.* When anything bad or negative happened between us, he always blamed ME! He could not handle anything, so he had to blame me. Since we were separated, he could not blame me anymore, even though he probably still did.

What gave him the right to take his sadness and frustration out on his eight-year-old daughter who was in distress?

I held my daughter, hugging her tight and soothing her. I told her that she has a right to her feelings and that it was OK to feel sad or homesick and that it was NOT right for her father to blame her or get angry with her for it.

Really, when I thought about it, I wondered who the adult was in this situation.

Just because his children did not function like toy soldiers and actually needed support and soothing, like most children do, just because they did not feel comfortable at his place, did NOT give him the right to hurt them.

I realized that I had been on the receiving end of his lack of empathy for far too long and, also, that I would <u>not</u> allow him to blame the kids for his inadequacies.

Trying to talk to him did not help, as he always acted as if he did nothing wrong.

All I could do after that incident was strengthen my children and myself. I let them know they would and will always be safe with me, and they could always express their thoughts and emotions when they were at home.

I could not change their dad, though. No matter how hard it hurt, they were meant to learn to get to know him for who he was.

When my ex and I were still married, I had tried to buffer his behavior for them. I provided an emotional bridge or an excuse for their dad. "Dad has to work, please do not disturb him," was the phrase I used every weekend. Now that we weren't together any longer, this bridge was no longer there. He had to handle their emotions himself.

I was saddened for my children and, of course, feared that my ex would emotionally abuse them.

During that time, I was there for them for 12 days and then they were with him for two days and then back to me for the next 12. The longer stretches that they were at home with me seemed like enough time to stock up on love and understanding.

As it turned out, they decided on their own that they did not want to visit him very much longer, which was only understandable.

It was time to put the ball back in his court.

He was the adult, if he wanted to see his children, he should have acted like a caring parental figure, like someone who understood and loved his children. Unfortunately, a caring, supportive attitude just didn't seem to be in his nature.

Luckily enough, no matter how the children's father handled their emotions, they knew that they would always have me on their side and that they were safe with me. I would be their anchor and safe haven as long as needed.

Emotions are as valid as your thoughts. You can't always put mind over matter – especially when you are an eight-year-old child.

My ex's lack of sympathy on this occasion was an eye-opening moment for me. I realized how easily I had taken on the responsibility for everything when we were together, and I, myself, always found fault for our issues within myself. I was so busy pleasing him that I never once considered that he might be wrong to blame me.

It was time for me to see his faults and no longer allow myself to be blamed for his shortcomings and flaws.

This realization was one giant step on my journey to being me.

Wisdom from within:

One thing that helped me when dealing with my ex was to put up my hands like a shield. I did this every time I got an email from him.

I used this to keep my distance and not get drawn into his attempts to blame me.

Another tactic that I used often, was to shower everyone in love. To do this:

- Put your hands on your heart.
- Breathe in deeply.
- Connect with your heart and the love within.
- Spread the love, let it flow out of your heart into every cell of your body.
- Share it with all your loved ones, all your neighbors and area.
- Then spread it over to your whole country, continent and the whole wide world.
- I even send some love to my ex, just to help clear his patterns.

Sharing the love is a wonderful tool to bring peace into our hearts and let the Universe handle the rest. Love is our true essence and love heals everything.

♥

FIRST WEEKEND WITHOUT KIDS

Do you have any memories of your first weekend alone, without the kids?

Oh, I remember it well. It was so hard. As I mentioned before, I spent the first weekend the kids were at their dad's with my friends at the spa. The next weekend he picked up the kids was approaching and this time I chose to stay at home alone.

I was looking forward to sleeping in and just being on my own to rest and recharge. I was looking forward to making the best of it. It felt good to have no obligations, no need to prepare any meals or be there for anyone.

However, everything turned out differently, as it usually does.

Toni picked the kids up on Friday, and all three were happy to stay with their dad for the weekend.

I stayed home and cried. I remember sitting in the chair, listening to music. All I could find was a Christmas CD, so I listened to Christmas music in March. It didn't matter to me. I just needed something to cut the silence.

I had a glass or two of wine and cried as it all sunk in. That was it. I would be alone every other weekend and Toni was really gone. I was alone. I truly felt for the first time that I was a single mom and would be for the rest of my life. I felt the brokenness of our family; we were no billboard family any longer. I saw my dream shatter, my dream of a happy family: father, mother, and children. It ended with the separation.

I probably had a bit too much wine, as I did not sleep so well. I remember I woke up early and I didn't feel well.

I started talking down to myself: Why did I have to drink so much wine – nearly a whole bottle – so I slept poorly the one time I could sleep?

I was still very harsh on myself back then. Nowadays I've learned to be gentler and more understanding of myself, too. I treat myself like I would any friend or one of my children – with compassion and understanding.

So, on that weekend long ago, I woke up feeling upset and hung over. To top it off, I had an email from Toni waiting for me.

He wrote about not getting a bonus we'd been expecting and told me that our financial situation was very bad. Either we had to take the kids out of school or sell our house.

I was shocked and devastated. I felt humiliated and yes, I was eager to do anything necessary to keep us afloat. However, there was this tiny voice that asked, *"Why me? Why do I have to be the one to make sacrifices?"*

He was the one creating extra expenses by living in a very expensive flat and heading two households. He was the one who wanted to move out in the first place.

Plus, why should the kids suffer more? They just lost the security of their father being at home. I did not want to pluck them out of their school or uproot them more by moving house right now.

So, resistance settled in along with fear, the deep fear for our survival, for safety, the fear of utter devastation.

I knew I wanted the best for my kids and I had to hold my ground, but how could I do this?

Of course, my first weekend on my own was totally ruined. I could not sleep the next night because I was so fearful about our future and stressed out; it took me months to get over it. I did not sleep well the whole time.

I broke out in hives. I woke in the middle of the night and my whole body itched. I nearly fell asleep when I was taking the children to school a couple of times, till I said no more. The safety of my children was at stake here. I finally got some herbal remedies to ease my stress.

As the weeks grew into months, we were not evicted from our home and the kids were still at the school. I could start breathing again.

I also had a worst-case scenario plan ready, just in case. This helped me to see, no matter what, we could all move to my mom's and have a roof over our head. Somehow, there would always be a way to survive. Luckily, we did not need to move in with my mother; however, having that option brought a bit of peace to my mind so I could rest and take care of the children.

I also realized that Toni did nothing to rein in his expenses, so I wondered why any financial deficit always landed on my shoulders.

I saw how he manipulated me. He shared bad news with me in order to try to get me to feel like the kids and I had to cut back on our spending, so he did not have to curb his. He was still dining at the most expensive places; he was still driving a sports car; he was still going on vacations; and yes, he was still shopping at designer boutiques. When I mentioned this to him, he simply said that he needed new suits and he deserved it all.

All of a sudden, I saw it clearly. *He* never wanted to live more frugally. He always meant to continue on as he always had; however, it was HIS decision to move out and, in order to make it work, he expected the kids to suffer.

Oh no! That was not going to work with me, so I learned to put my foot down and speak clearly. I stated that the kids would remain at their school – that this was nonnegotiable – and we would stay in our house as the kids needed stability, so they could deal with everything else that was going on.

And you know what? He accepted it. Now that I had clarity in my own situation, he went along with it as well. Still, every now and then, he came moaning about the expenses, but I felt he could do better. It was on him to rein in his own luxurious expenses, not cut from our necessities.

I fought for my children. Without them, I know I would have been lost. I did not feel worthy of any of it; however, I knew the children deserved the stability they needed to process the changes in our lives.

Standing up for my children taught me to stand up for myself. It took me years to learn that I was (and am) worthy. However, this first weekend on my own taught me so much about how manipulative Toni could be and how he just handed all of his worries to me. I was the one who wasn't able to sleep because of the financial stress. He, on the other hand, slept sound and deep because he just shoveled the stress onto me.

I vowed that weekend that I would not check my emails during my weekends off, especially not the ones from Toni, as I knew he would just dump his dirt on to try to get a reaction or ruin my time alone.

Learning to be assertive in what I allowed to come my way was one big step and lesson. Having him ruin that weekend and turn it into a weekend from hell, so to speak, taught me about how Toni operated and how to handle him in the future.

Wisdom from within:

Enjoy being OFFline. The need to constantly be available can be stressful.

When out in nature, put your phone on flight mode, so you can still take photos while enjoying your time in nature without being interrupted.

Take a day off away from your computer every now and then. Your body and soul will thank you for it.

Remember you deserve time by yourself.

Find ways you love to recharge and do them regularly.

♥

HE JUST KNOWS THE RIGHT THINGS TO SAY

How important is emotional intelligence to you?

For me, it was always important to be with someone who was knowledgeable and well educated. I love to talk about more than just the weather.

It was only around the time of my break up that I learned about emotional intelligence, though. I read about it in regard to raising children and how it plays a role in their development. Yes, I found that emotional intelligence was so very important to me and for me; it is an important part of a well-rounded person's character.

Toni was (and still is) a very intelligent person. He went to university and did intensive studies. He knew a lot about a good variety of topics and could also recite facts by heart. He was very good at memorizing details.

I knew he was not a very emotional person, though. He did not allow himself to express feelings openly, or so it seemed. He relied mostly on his intellect and knowledge he learned from books.

So, shortly after our separation, my sister-in-law came to visit. I felt it was important for the children to remain in contact with their aunt and she and I were good friends. However, I found out later that blood was thicker than water in our case and she sided more with her brother, which is understandable. I think this is only natural and part of going through a breakup. Friends take sides, family members take sides, and both people end up with good friends and people to support them through their lives. That is very much OK and actually a great cleansing of one's social circle. You don't want people over sharing or being indiscreet with your ex.

Back to emotional intelligence: I remember distinctly how my sister-in-law and I stood in the kitchen and there was another person there who mentioned that Toni missed the kids. I felt a bit sad for Toni, thinking it must be hard not being around his own kids. I had a glimmer of hope that, yes, he actually cared after all! Maybe being separated from the kids brought him around to it. Maybe the saying, "Distance makes the heart grow fonder" was right in his case? Maybe there was hope on the horizon. However, because of my experience with him, I doubted his statement very much and instinctively felt that he was just saying it for the benefit of looking good.

My sister-in-law looked at me, and said, "He sure knows what to say"!

Somehow, this insight really opened the door for me to see him clearly. Yes, I thought, in one of the books it mentioned that a father was supposed to miss his kids, so that's why he was saying it to others. However, simply saying it because it's the right thing to say did not make it right or true.

I realized at that moment that Toni got his intelligence from books. Like his sister pointed out, he knew the right things to say. He tried to connect with everyone by saying the right thing, and yes, it worked on me 20 years earlier. I remember how he said the right things when we were dating; however, I also realized that I never really connected with him on a heart or spiritual level. I realized that day that his emotions were never really there to begin with. For him, it was just empty words. Using the right words did not make him an emotionally intelligent person.

At that instant, I realized what I was missing all those years: a true soul connection, true emotional empathy, true love, and understanding.

When my sister-in-law formulated, in words, what my heart knew for years it all became clear: my ex really didn't have emotional intelligence that matched his book smarts. Somehow, he knew the right words to use to impress people; however, he didn't seem capable of actually emoting the feelings.

Having this clarity helped me release my guilt about him not seeing the kids. It helped me to see that he and I were incompatible. It was time to see my own worth, time to realize that I was the more intelligent person in this parenting partnership – at least in the way my kids needed at the time. I was, indeed, better than he was at some things. For so long, I had swept my value under the carpet. I downgraded myself in the past for being emotional to begin with. Now I saw that my emotional intelligence was just as valuable as his studies.

Recognizing these characteristics within me that were so valuable, so important to me as a person, and also monumental to how I dealt with my children as a mother was liberating. This was one small step toward reconnecting with my worth.

Hooray! I finally felt good about myself. I could see that the world needed me, even though my world back then only consisted of my three children.

I could teach them about emotions and how important it was (and is) to acknowledge and express one's feelings. Pushing things down never helps and emotions are part of our whole being, just like rational and intellectual thoughts are.

So yes, emotional intelligence became even more important to my thoughts about others and myself, too. Without it, one can never be a well-rounded person.

Toni used to say, "Mind over matter." I can see now that he lives according to this theory; however, I do not. I am such a heart-centered person. I finally know that an emotionally intelligent person is just as valuable as an intellectually intelligent person. Back then, I undermined myself by looking up to Toni so much. Learning to see things from a different perspective and learning how we all are different, and learning to accept each person as she is has helped me to accept myself just the way I am. I am valuable.

Wisdom from within:

Look at yourself as if you were your very best friend. Look at yourself from the outside. What do you see?

Observe and notice. See yourself through the eyes of your best friend, of your children, or of beloved family members.

See all the good things they see; see how valuable you are to them.

Breathe in how valuable you are, as you are.

Be grateful for being you.

Smile at yourself for being you.

You are worthy, just the way you are.

You are worthy, by just being you.

♥

LOST IN THE LIVING ROOM

Were there any special light bulb or Aha! moments you experienced?

Yes, there were several. At times, I felt like an explosion of shooting stars from all of the inspiration and insights I received after Toni and I split up.

One discovery in particular, though, was like an epiphany. It was a true wake up call, one I will always remember. It was deeply humbling and showed me what a people pleaser I had been during the 20 years I spent with this man.

I remember distinctly it was March. Spring was in the air, and spring was starting for my life as well. I was already starting on my new life: life after marriage, life without my husband, life as an "official" single mom (*officially* single, considering the fact that I had already been taking care of the kids mostly on my own, even when we were married).

So, I was in my living room, sitting on a chair, contemplating life in general and my life in particular. It finally sunk in… I am alone, this is it and this is my life now, just me.

I sat in my chair looking around my living room with fresh eyes.

I looked at the settees made of white leather. I looked at them and said, "This is not me!"

I looked around some more. I looked at the rugs lying on the floors. I looked at them and said, "This is not me!"

Then I looked at the bookshelves lining the walls and at the books they held. Colorful leather-bound books filled a huge wall and shelves around the room. I looked at them and said, "This is not me!"

I looked at the prints hanging on the walls. I looked at them and said, "This is not me!"

I looked around and looked some more and then finally it hit me: nothing in my house was *me*. Nothing represented my true essence.

I did not like the white leather sofas, which made me feel cold when I sat on them. They were so slippery I nearly fell off of them sometimes, and they made me feel like I lived in a museum.

I did not like the rugs on the floor, expensive Persian rugs that were OK, but not really my taste.

I looked at the books, books Toni started collecting well before we met and kept collecting through our marriage, the books we had to move from one flat to another, the books that traveled with us around the world. The books that always made Toni look so intelligent, and the books everyone was in awe of. The books that felt so heavy and suffocating, the books I was not allowed to touch as the gold writing could come off onto my hands when I held them. NO, those were clearly NOT my books.

The paintings on the walls were OK, but they were my ex's taste in art, not my own.

Nothing in my house represented *me*! Looking around more frantically, I collapsed in my seat again and asked:

BUT WHAT *IS* ME? WHO AM I?

I realized at that moment that I had lost myself. I had completely lost myself in the marriage and being a mom and I had no idea who I was anymore.

Yes, Toni was older than me. I was only 20 when I met him, so it was simply natural that I let him take over.

I did not care what kind of sofas we had. I was happy enough with leather because it was easy to wipe up after little kids.

I thought it was OK to have some rugs to cover the wooden floors and give some warmth.

I love books, but I love paperbacks and books I can read and touch and use.

Pictures were good, too. It is always great to have some color on the walls.

So, I know I didn't mind having many of these items. As a couple, you compromise and find something that both like.

However, there was nothing, nothing in this room that represented my tastes and ME.

I was astonished. When I looked around, tears came to my eyes, and I wondered if this was my legacy, being the woman who didn't mind? The woman who didn't really care? The woman who had no opinion?

And then it all started. I asked myself, "what *would* I like?" I didn't really know and that made me sad. I realized that I forgot what I, myself, liked during the last 20 years of my life.

I sat there thinking that I would turn 40 in August, and that, at 40, I had no idea who I was anymore. How bizarre was that?

I also realized that I had been together with that man for 20 years, so HALF my life. I gave half my life to this man, and I felt like I lost half my life. It felt devastating, like a part of me was missing and lost forever.

At that moment, I looked at the pictures and thought, "What do I like?" I remembered that I loved Monet, a beautiful impressionist painter. I loved the colors he used, his style, the flowers, and themes. I remembered that I went to a museum as a teenager and loved his paintings.

So yes, I was gonna get myself some Monet love! Posters, of course!

I also remembered that I had a Tinguely poster as a teen and loved it. Somewhere in between the moves, it got tossed. What a pity. Oh well, I would get a new one of those as well!

It felt good. I was infusing myself with love and life and got an idea of who I was and what I liked again.

Then I looked around my living room and felt uncomfortable as it felt more like a museum than a home. I decided to move around the furniture a bit to bring in some fresh energy and also to find out how I liked it to be arranged.

I was coming back to life and a breeze of fresh air was blowing through my soul.

As for books, I remembered what kind of books I loved to read and ordered some from Amazon. When the paperbacks I ordered came in, I was ready to put them on the shelves, and I also decided to send the leather books to my ex, as they were part of who he was, but not at all a part of me. It felt good to get rid of those books.

This was the story of my life then. I was ready to start fresh.

The moment I had that day, sitting in the chair realizing that I had no idea who I was anymore, still hits me deeply. It was a huge turning point for me. After that, I allowed myself to explore and rekindle with my own essence, my own truth.

I often had to go back to my teenage years, the time before I met my husband, to know what I really liked, or connect with the things I liked back then. For example, I didn't really know what kind of music I liked anymore. When I was driving in the car I listened to the radio broadcasting the newest songs. When we were traveling with Toni, however, he always and only listened to classical music.

It was the same at home. I didn't really like to have music on at home because I loved the quiet, but he always put on music, which was OK. I didn't mind his classical music, however, since my epiphany, the question became about what music I preferred. I remembered that I loved Genesis, Eric Clapton, and Joe Cocker, among others, prior to my marriage. Luckily, I had iTunes and was able to download some of my favorite music easily. Listening to this music helped me remember Caroline, and feel the essence of who I was.

So, by going back to my teenage years, I was able to hook on to what I loved back then and transfer that into the present. I also started listening more to the radio and noticing what music I liked that was being played there.

I still had to catch up over 20 years, but it felt so good to finally know what I liked and explore it in my own way.

The next time I needed a sofa, I walked around the furniture store and sat on several. I chose something that was comfortable, not just practical, as my kids were older by then and I wouldn't have to clean up so many spills.

"It is never too late to become the person you could have been." (Quote by George Elliot)

Becoming true to myself and rekindling the fire of my essence has helped me a lot in making decisions. Also, the realization that I can now decide on my own, that there are no more compromises, and there is no husband who has to agree with my choice or like what I choose helps as well.

It is just me now, and yes, of course, the children, who I often involved in decision-making. I'm teaching them that it is important to have an opinion and that it is OK to find out what you truly want and like.

This was a huge epiphany, don't you agree? It was one of the major turning points in my life after my marriage ended. This was the wake-up call from the, "don't mind anything, slumbering, I have no true opinion, you choose" kind of Caroline to a Caroline who knows who she is, what she likes, and who is ready to make her own decisions for her life.

Wisdom from within:

I love the movie, *Runaway Bride*, with Julia Roberts. She always said she liked her eggs the way her fiancée did, until she had time to learn how she liked her eggs.

How do you like your eggs?

What else in your life can do with a little more you?

In what areas of life do you not have an opinion? Why?

Tap into yourself. Feel what is right for you and go with it.

Remember to take it one step at a time.

♥

SNAKE BITE

What was the darkest moment in your journey so far?

One of my darkest moments must have been when little Horatio, who was only five years old at the time, had a very bad experience with the new woman in his dad's life. I am still wondering how any human being can mistreat a child as she did, and why the heck my ex didn't intervene and protect our child in the first place?

I know it is always hard to trust others with the safety and well-being of your children. I feel it is especially hard leaving them with your ex and the new woman in his life. There is nothing so devastating as to learn that your little one was handled much more roughly than I was comfortable with while visiting his dad.

My mom sometimes feared the kids might love Jane more than me. I never worried about that; I knew that I was *Mom* and my kids loved me, but I never imagined that they would have to fear their stepmother.

I never treated Jane as the Wicked Stepmom prior to this incident. I never imagined, either, that she would be so mean as to hurt my babies. She, through her actions, earned the title of Wicked Stepmother.

So, here's the story of the *Snake Bite*:

One weekend, during the early days of our separation, my three kids came home very subdued from a weekend at their Dad's. Horatio was especially melancholy.

I took him in my arms and we sat down together. He sat on my lap, facing me, and I cradled him. He started to cry, and I just held him and rocked, him sending love.

Eventually, he started to open up to me about why he was crying.

He said, "She hurt me!"

"She what!? Who?" I asked, trying to calm myself, while I was nearly jumping out of my skin, ready to attack.

I remembered kids might over exaggerate, and Horatio was only five so lots of things might theoretically hurt him. I took a deep breath and tried to focus on him without my imagination going wild.

So, he started to tell me his story:

They were eating lunch and Jane was telling them about something the kids do call a "Snake Bite." Horatio had no idea what a Snake Bite was, likely, he hadn't learned that yet at school, so Jane was *kind enough* to get up, walk over, and show him!

She showed him – not like any normal adult would do – like maybe slowly twisting his arm, but not really squeezing and in no way hurting the child, just giving him an idea about how someone did a Snake Bite – but not causing the child any pain.

No. Jane went up to Horatio, took his arm and fully twisted it with a vengeance! Of course, Horatio cried out and was hurt. His arm was probably red and throbbing.

After he told me about the ordeal, I held him and told him that what she did was horrible, and I was very sorry he had to experience this.

Then his little voice said:

"Mom, that was not the worst. The worst part of it was that Daddy only laughed!"

I was so shocked! How could Toni laugh? Why didn't he step up and tell his girlfriend that she was out of line?

Who, in their normal mind, would even do something like this to a five-year-old child?

I sat there, completely stunned, shook to the core and just held my little baby. I had no words. I could just console my little one, rock him, and make sure he felt safe again.

My heart was pounding. I was deeply hurt for my child.

Deeply worried, I reached out to Catherine and Mathew, who just nodded their heads. "Yes," they said, "we can still hear him cry. It was awful."

I looked at my older two kids thinking what fabulous Empaths they were. They could truly feel for their younger brother.

They told me that Horatio was shrieking and crying so hard that they could still remember it much later. It shook them to the core, seeing their little brother being hurt by their stepmom.

What could I do to keep my children safe? What could I have done, when I wasn't even there? I knew worrying wouldn't help.

Sitting there, knowing that this new woman in their lives – a woman who came around to our house for play dates with her two girls, a woman I felt was a colleague of mine – was actually hurting my kids. Why? How?

I still can't understand how *any* woman could hurt a little child on purpose. Maybe she even enjoyed doing a full-on Snake Bite on a little boy's arm.

What did I learn from this? First of all, I was deeply humbled that all three of my kids trusted me enough to share this frightening story with me and that Horatio felt safe enough to come home and let the tears flow.

I also learned, at that moment, that the father of my children didn't have the wellbeing of our kids as his highest priority. He seemed more concerned about keeping his new woman happy.

What a disaster. What should we do from now on?

It was a new start for us. I encouraged my children to be more assertive, while also trusting them to come to me with anything that happened to them.

It was wonderful. We established "safety protocols," like they could go to the neighbor's and ring the doorbell, call me, or even 911 if anything like that happened again.

I know I was able to empower my children, despite my – or maybe because of my – astonishment over what happened.

I learned, with my children, to stand up for what is right, and that no one can or should treat any one of us unkindly or even hurt us on purpose.

I also realized that the wellbeing of my children was more important to me than having them see their father.

I learned that I could trust my instincts and trust my kids. Even though I knew this woman for a while, I never felt close to her. Now I know why.

I also realized that my children and I sit on the sensitive side of the spectrum. Our senses and perceptions are different from many others and it is 100% OK not to follow the idealized version of the rules. Still, my ex and his new woman should have respected Horatio's feelings either way, and she should have been much more careful with him, as I feel any normal grown woman would be.

After this episode, I created my own method of "shared" parenting, always keeping the wellbeing of my kids at the center of it all. The children and their safety were more important than the rights of a father who I felt wasn't making fatherhood a priority.

And I accepted that they might not feel safe at their dad's and eventually allowed them to skip visitation if they didn't feel like going to see him.

Neither the email I wrote Toni about this incident nor the discussion with the child psychologists helped resolve the issue. He probably still thinks that there was nothing wrong with what Jane did to Horatio. I tried to explain it to him – as did the experts – but his thoughts about it remained the same.

No, our kids never seemed to be high on his list of priorities. Why could I ever think that he would change after we separated?

I started to see him as a selfish person, which was a turning point in my freedom. I could let go of trying to please him, as he just did and thought what he wanted when he wanted, anyway.

I could allow myself to be a bit more assertive with him after that, too. Stepping up for my children taught me to step up for myself as well.

I also learned to trust my own instincts more. My good judgment of what was right and wrong was on target, and I saw the kids had a good sense of it, too.

After that, I was less inclined to trust and listen to Toni's idea of what was right or wrong, and yes, I did not take his input at face value after that. I saw, for the first time, that he didn't seem to have sympathy toward others.

After this incident, I somehow started to feel good about myself again. I was not a total failure. I saw and felt more than he did. I think I started to stand up taller in that moment. I unfolded myself like a gentle little flower started to bloom within me. I felt good for finally standing for my own feelings and I felt like, "*Yes, I am on the right path.*"

For me, years of neglect, years of not feeling like I was good enough, years of accepting someone else's opinion without questioning were finally coming to an end. A new era had started: a time where I learned to listen within myself again. This is something that we all should be doing, but some of us – those who are dealing with people like Toni – might have forgotten. I hope my experience helps them to remember as well.

Wisdom from within:

I love to ask the Universe and the Angels for help with my earthly problems. I always ask Archangel Michael to protect my children, whenever they go out. I also love to call on the support of Archangel Metatron, as he is the archangel who looks after children and their caregivers.

It feels good to share the responsibility of bringing up children when you're on your own. With the help of the angels, all is well.

We can't always be there for our kids. Sending helpers along with them and also knowing that we all have guardian angels has helped me to let them go and trust that they will be safe.

♥

GUILT

Did I ever feel guilty?

Of course, I felt guilty throughout the process of my divorce. I felt guilty about not being able to make things work out. I felt guilty that my kids had to go through this when they were so young.

To be honest, there were moments before this – many moments – I wanted to walk away from my marriage. There were times I wanted to leave my ex-husband; however, I didn't want to put my children through that experience. How could I drag my kids through a divorce? How could I take them away from their dad?

Guilt and exhaustion kept me from walking out of a very unhappy marriage, in which I tried to please my husband to make him happy. I didn't really understand that I never could be the source of his happiness, anyway. No one can make someone else happy. I know that now.

Witnessing what my kids went through during the separation and divorce was devastating. I was so very sad for them. I felt their pain. I wished I could have prevented it all.

Indeed, I often sat there and let my thoughts wander. "What if I just tried harder? What if I was nicer? What if I told him he could stay? What if? If only…" All those "what if's" were corroding my confidence and I knew that I needed to face reality and walk away from those hurtful thoughts.

I remember one evening when I was in bed reading one of my spiritual books like I often did. I dwelled on the inspiration and thought of those times as the precious moments in my days. I treasured the little escapes and peaceful times the books and their words provided for me. While reading, I came upon a sentence in the book that said something to the effect that *children choose their parents before they are born*. They don't just choose their parents, either, but they choose the situations and experiences they will live through when they come to earth.

Wow. I let this sink in a little. If this was true – and I felt it to be in every cell of my body, there was this pull of it, the pull that said I unearthed a serious truth – this would mean that my three kids *chose* the experience of this separation and their heartbreak when they chose to be born into their lives.

I sat there with the book on my lap, and it was like a huge weight has shifted off my shoulders and chest. I blinked my eyes. My heart was pounding. I swallowed hard. Wow. After this revelation, I could finally breathe freely. Could it truly be all that simple?

All of a sudden, I could see our struggles through fresh eyes.

My three amazing, wonderful children actually came here to experience going through this divorce. Wow! So that meant it was not my fault.

I could accept the situation we were facing on a whole new level. I realized that it was all meant to be, and that, no matter how much I bent over backward to make it work with my ex, it would still have come out the same. My kids had chosen to go through this separation and divorce, no matter how painful the experience was for them. They were meant to endure this. On a soul level, they wanted to go through this.

This was it. It was all meant to be, so I didn't need to fight against it any longer?

I cried. Tears were running down my cheeks. This realization allowed me to release so much guilt. It felt so deeply liberating and my heart opened. I embraced my kids with all my heart right there, sitting alone in my bed with the book on my lap. I had found peace.

This one eye-opening moment was a shift in perception, a big change in the way I saw the whole process. I did not see my kids as poor little victims or puppets anymore. I saw them as spiritual souls, as wise souls, and wonderful companions in this game of life we chose to play together.

You might laugh, but it felt like this whole separation experience was just a game the Universe put in front of us. I could finally embrace it as the experience it was meant to be. It no longer felt like a devastating catastrophe we couldn't free ourselves from. It felt more like a path we had to walk, rather than a situation we were stuck in.

When the guilt washed away, I was able to think of my children with fresh love and understanding. I could truly be there for them to support them and guide them, instead of wishing things were different. I didn't have to continue to try to wish this experience away.

Accepting the situation we are all in, with no one at fault, was heartwarming. It freed me of my *what ifs* and opened the way to a new us. My life with my children had truly begun. We were four souls on a shared and special spiritual path.

Wisdom from within:

I love to read books by Diana Cooper; I feel they carry so much wisdom in them.

Through reading her work and that of Louise L. Hay, I also learned to say to myself: "I accept you Caroline!" – a very liberating affirmation.

You can play creating your own affirmation of acceptance, by trying out phrases like:

I accept you fully, Caroline.

I accept you just the way you are, Caroline.

The way you are is just fine, Caroline.

Acceptance plays such a big role in our lives. Have fun playing with accepting yourself and your situations.

♥

YOU'D BETTER BEHAVE

Were there any scary moments?

There were plenty of scary moments, especially when I was not sure my kids were safe at their dad's house. I remember the times they told me he had a glass of whiskey or had drunk a glass or two of wine before he drove them home. We were lucky nothing ever happened.

However, a scarier moment was when Catherine told me what Jane did to her while Daddy was not watching.

They all had dinner together and it might have been louder or less formal than usual – like a family dinner with children. Kids are kids, after all.

Anyhow, when Toni went to the kitchen and turned his back on everyone, Jane grabbed Catherine's arm and pulled her close. She looked Catherine in the eye, and told her, "You'd better behave. I will be your Daddy's future wife!"

Catherine was shocked and scared.

When I heard about this incident, I was annoyed and shocked. How could Jane treat my little girl like this? Wasn't Jane an adult?

All I could do in that moment was to soothe my little girl and tell her that Daddy was still married to Mommy, so Jane had to wait for her turn.

I was silly enough to mention this incident to Toni. It was early times in our separation and I was still hoping he would have the children's safety in mind. Of course, he completely denied it. He even tried to accuse me of trying to manipulate the children.

Once again, he told me the kids were happy at his place and that I only wanted to hear bad stories from them. Little did he know that the kids could be calm and hold it together when they had to (like with him) and then finally relax back home, where they felt safe.

Toni told me, too, that he and Jane had no intention of marrying. Ha! They actually got married not even a year after he and I were divorced.

I still remember this incident and I feel Jane showed her real face as the Evil Stepmother once again.

I also realized that Jane wanted to put herself into a ready-made nest. She probably thought, "Oh Toni is earning big bucks, so I'd better catch him."

I felt she was just with him for the money.

I remember one time Catherine told me, "Yeah Mom, you married Dad for his money, too."

I had to laugh, and I explained to her that, when I met Toni 20 years prior, he was a nobody. He had only just started an office job after studying research at a university. He had no money – he was in debt – he couldn't even pay his taxes. So, no, I did not marry him for his money.

I felt I loved him. Maybe what I felt back then wasn't true love; however, it seemed like love to me in those days. He was the man I wanted to have children with (I wonder why now) and I could imagine the two of us sitting and reading together when we were old. Unfortunately, it turned out that my whole marriage felt like this – sitting together, reading, each one of us lost in our own little world – without passion, fun, or zest shared between us.

So, Jane came and took the foundations that Toni and I built away. She set herself up in a ready-made nest – a nest I helped build. I kept Toni's life stress-free so that he could pursue his career. I moved from one place to another, leaving my jobs and homes behind and then later dragging our kids along.

I used to say I was spending "his money." It took me a long time to realize it was OUR money. I was a big part of his success. I remember I kept saying, "I am just a mom!" when instead, I should have said, "I am a full-time domestic manager doing an amazing job with our three gorgeous children!"

Anyway, let's get back to the story. Yes, it was very scary for me knowing that Jane had the nerve to just grab my little girl and be vicious to her – especially behind Toni's back. How could I protect my children from a mean stepmom, especially when I was dealing with an oblivious ex-husband?

I did it the only way I could. I talked to my children, reassuring them that I would always be there for them when they needed to talk. I kept a line of communication wide open between them and me. I kept myself from freaking out. I stayed calm, trusting that all would be well, and I took one step at a time.

What did I learn? I learned to treasure myself more. I learned that I was willing to fight for what was rightfully mine. I grew stronger through all the stories my children relayed to me, while at the same time, I learned how mean, malicious, and calculating Jane could be. All of this made me even more aware that I was not fighting only for myself; I was fighting for my three children.

It brought out the bear mother in me. I was and am ready to defend my three cubs anytime. Gone is the shy and adaptable woman who married Toni and let things go, the Caroline who just accepted what she was offered. I was stronger – ready to stand up for my children and for myself as well.

Wisdom from within:

Grounding helps us to get back to ourselves, especially when we are dealing with scary things.

It's best to stand barefoot on grass, soil, or moss. If it's not possible to go outside, just imagine you are standing barefoot on grass. Then imagine how roots growing out of the soles of your feet, going deep down into Mother Earth's soil. Breathe loving and nurturing energy through your roots into your body.

Allowing yourself to connect to the loving and nurturing energy Mother Earth shares, breathing out all the worries and stress, helps you to grow stronger.

Imagine yourself being like the mighty oak tree. You are deeply rooted, with a firm trunk and flexible branches that are able to sway in the wind without toppling over.

♥

I CAN'T ACCEPT THE NEW SITUATION

Was there a time you could just simply not take it anymore?

Oh, there were so many times when I was just tired of dealing with everything related to my separation, divorce, and my ex and his new woman. Times I wanted the earth to open up and suck me in so I could just vanish. Other times, I was ready to throw myself on the floor and just have a good old temper tantrum. And of course, there were times I would have just loved to hide under my duvet and cry out of sheer exhaustion and frustration.

Then there were times I wanted to tear his head off or scream at him.

There was this one time when I just could not take it any longer, and I told him the truth, the plain truth, and nothing but the truth.

In hindsight, it was very bold of me and I sense this was the time he upped his game. It was good to see him speechless for once; it felt very liberating, indeed. I was standing up and speaking up, something that was very new for me (and him!) back then.

I remember sitting in the office of our child psychologists, both of them were present, and we were discussing the situation of our kids and how they could feel better when they visited their dad.

Toni was sitting in a posture designed to show he cared; his long, lean body slightly tilted forward. He seemed attentive and listening, nodding his head every now and then, his blond curls bobbing.

When the psychologist asked him what he thought about the situation around his kids and why they acted up at his place, he said:

"I know the kids have a hard time because their mother (me!) has not accepted the new situation!" He was referring to his relationship with Jane.

I nearly burst out laughing. How could he always twist it around, so it was my fault? How could he think everything was always just MY fault?

Once again, I was faced with the fact that he <u>always</u> put the blame on me. No matter what was happening, it was always somehow my fault.

I took a deep breath and calmly said:

"Actually, Toni, I am deeply grateful to Jane for freeing me from you!

I have never ever felt better! I lost over 10 kg in the last couple of months, I finally had great sex, and I feel good for the first time in forever! Thank you so much for leaving me!"

I still remember his stunned face. He was speechless. Yeah, I know he would have loved for me to be suffering because he left me. He never thought I could enjoy my freedom or that I would come to realize how suffocated and neglected I was with him.

I went on, "I don't care what you or Jane are doing; however, how you deal with my kids is very much my concern!"

Even though the child psychologist congratulated me on speaking my truth and stepping up, I know that day changed the course of it all. Toni was out for revenge after that. I am not sure he ever felt guilty about leaving me for another woman, or whether he hoped I would miss him dearly, I didn't know. However, I knew the gloves came off that day, and I received punch after punch from then on, as the coming stories will show.

What did I learn from this all? I learned that it is very liberating to speak the truth. I was so relieved that I didn't have to walk on eggshells around him any longer. I also truly felt that everything was going to be OK, that my life without Toni was a better life for me. I realized how true to myself I could be, and I reconnected with the inner, mischievous Caroline a bit – the young girl who climbed trees, jumped over fences, and had a lot of fun and adventure. Gone was the people-pleasing, all-understanding, picture-perfect Caroline.

I also realized that divorce could be a marathon event. No matter who *won* each sprint, endurance and being true to myself were the keys to this game.

I felt I set new boundaries. I did not accept Toni's pseudo psycho rambling anymore. I knew my feelings were right. The kids did not feel well when they were with him and it had nothing to do with me.

To be honest, I always wondered whether I might have unknowingly influenced the kids; if I subconsciously did not want them to keep seeing their dad just because I felt uneasy or hurt. However, that encounter showed me clearly that Toni was more eager to put the blame on me, rather than looking inwards and finding ways to make his kids more at ease himself.

While I felt I looked far too much within myself to find faults, I realized that Toni looked outside to blame me. This dynamic had made us a great match when we were together, but I just wasn't willing to have it any longer.

It was time to change this pattern for the better. I knew, full well, I could never make him look into his own behavior for answers; however, I could stop blaming myself for everything. I started on that day. I was ready to start MY life.

Wisdom from within:

If I find myself surrounded by negative people, I usually surround myself in beautiful loving pink light.

I imagine beautiful pink light wrapping all around me, from head to toe, and as wide as my arms can reach when I stretch them out. I also love to shower myself with rose petals in my visions.

Of course, real rose petals also help us to keep a higher vibration. You can scatter some around your home, put in your bath water, or spray rose scented room spray on your bed.

If the person I have to meet is a gossip or complains a lot, like my ex blaming me, I just imagine their speech is going into a bucket of salt water. I see it like in cartoons, a speech bubble going into the water; whatever the person is saying gets cleansed. Then it does not affect me, plus I can get what they want to say without all the negativity attached. This helps me feel like a better listener.

Have fun playing with this.

♥

FOUR GIRLS AGAINST HORATIO

Do you feel like it was just all too much for the children sometimes?

Oh yes, definitely. I mean, they had the normal childhood changes to go through, plus the adaptation necessary to get used to the separation, and then spending two weekends per month at their dad's, where everything was so different from home. They needed to learn their way around so many new situations.

There were a couple of times when I wanted to pull the plug on visitation, when I felt that Toni was not considerate enough towards his own children.

As mentioned in another chapter, he moved to his new apartment around March and the kids visited him there every other weekend. One weekend in June, he picked them up for what, at first, seemed like a normal visit. On the way to his house, he told them that there would be a surprise for them waiting at his apartment.

The kids had no idea what would hit them that Friday evening. The suspense caused pure pandemonium.

That particular weekend, they arrived at their dad's new home, where they had only spent a couple of weekends, to face a brand new and overwhelming situation. Without Toni having warned them, Jane had moved in with her two girls.

As if that wasn't enough to handle, they had houseguests that weekend, on top of it all.

Can you imagine? It was such a great shock for my three. Not only did they not have much time with their dad since he moved out, now everything was way different at his house.

Catherine found that she had to sleep in the girls' room on a mattress on the floor; she complained how uncomfortable this old mattress was every time she came home afterward. Plus, she was downgraded to just a guest in her own father's home.

The boys had to camp in the living room, as their room was taken over by the guests. All in all, there were about eight to ten kids staying over for the whole weekend.

Do I have to share how they felt after this weekend? You can imagine how upsetting this all was. I still wonder how Toni could try to sell this as a surprise to his own children? He was very removed from reality, I would say, and really not considerate towards his own kids. How could he overwhelm our children like that knowing they had just gone through a break-up?

It was also the deathblow to their hope that maybe Daddy might come back. It was now official: he had a new woman – not only a girlfriend, but also a new family.

From then on, it was a roller coaster ride. There were weekends when they were barely tolerated in the house and then there were others where they were simply ignored, left to their own devices.

Yes, Mathew just hid behind the computer, which did not help his mood when he came back home. However, it was probably best for him to just stay away from all the noise and chaos going on in his dad's home. Mathew was a very sensitive child (you can read more in my E-book, *My Life with an Indigo Child,* available on my website, http://palmyhealing.com) He hid many weekends at the computer, not feeling safe.

Catherine was sometimes happy to have "sisters" around, girls she could collaborate with. It helped her to have friends to go against her brothers. There was also another girl living in another flat in the same building. All of the girls were about the same age, so the four of them had a fabulous time, most of the time, at least.

But the four girls teamed up against Horatio. Catherine might have felt good when it was happening, but often felt guilty later at home. She might not have behaved so cruelly toward her little brother if she hadn't been with a group of other girls.

I understand Horatio wanted to be part of the team, too. His older brother was hiding at the computer and he had no one to play with. He was only five years old and he was very social, on top of it all.

However, the girls did not want him in their group. It was likely too, that Horatio was trying to get their attention with childlike behavior or by simply intruding on them. There are many ways he could have let everyone know he felt left out and, as annoying as he could be, he was still a young boy who needed attention.

Where were his dad and girlfriend?

From what I heard, they were just absent, not only emotionally, but also in their parental supervision. They were happy when the kids were off their shoulders, so to speak.

The children told me that they even locked themselves in their bedroom every afternoon for their "*nap.*"

One time, Horatio fell off the trampoline (not something I felt a five-year-old child should be using without supervision, anyway, especially not with other kids on it too) and hurt his foot. He went to Daddy's door and knocked, only to be told by Jane: "Go away, we are napping!"

Luckily, he was just a bit bruised. It was nothing that a bit of Arnica and Mom's love and cuddles couldn't heal after he returned from the weekend.

Can you imagine if something serious had happened? Really, accidents happen all the time and it seemed as if the adults were too busy hiding out, instead of stepping up to their parental duties to supervise the kids and be there for them. Yes, parenthood is a full-time job, 24/7, especially with young children. You can't just block them out. And really, Toni had them a total of four days a month. It wasn't such a burden to him.

Horatio started to refuse to go to visit his dad, which was understandable. He was teased and bullied and mistreated by four girls and no one stepped in to defend him. It must have felt awful for a five-year-old little boy to feel so helpless and alone.

Hearing those stories from my children made me realize that Toni had made it very easy for himself. I was not a helicopter mom, but I still felt I needed to be near or at least reachable when several kids were playing together. For me, it was important that they played nicely and were not mean to each other. And, of course, I wanted to be there in the case some odd accident happened that required immediate attention.

It's OK to take a step back and let children's conflicts play out by themselves, and there are times when you need to step in. However, you have to be observant and present for your children.

It was no wonder that I always felt exhausted. Being a mom is hard work. Being constantly tuned into what the kids were doing and what was going on was tiring; however, it was necessary to keep the children safe and sound, even more so when other children are over.

I know we hear stories of men passing on childcare duties or having an easier time with their children; however, what is the sense of having visitation with your own children when you are not really present for their visit at all? I feel strongly that, to build a relationship with your children, you need to engage with them and do fun things together. It is important to interact with your children when they are visiting you – especially after a divorce or separation.

It seemed as if Toni and Jane felt it was more important that they had their naptime and were able to escape the children. Why? The kids were only spending two days out of every two weeks with them. They had their privacy and their time together for the other twelve days. Why couldn't Toni make an effort to truly be with his kids?

I still don't know whether he just was eager to hide from his kids or whether Jane was behind it. It doesn't really matter, as he was an eager participant in ignoring his own children when they were with him. Of course, he complained later that the kids did not want to come see him. He could not imagine why. He said he had no idea.

I didn't have to wonder. I knew why the kids rightly refused to go to their dad's. Hearing their stories, knowing what they went through when they visited, and seeing how completely exhausted they felt every time they came home gave me ample reason. I knew I had to rely on my own judgment.

The books tell you how important it is for the children to see their estranged father regularly; however, Toni didn't make time for them when they were at his house and he always wanted me to make special arrangements with him.

For the safety of my children also for their emotional wellbeing, it was OK that they stayed with me all of the time. I left the door open and they were able to visit their dad when they wanted to. However, they needed a break from visiting him, which was very understandable.

I learned that every situation is unique, and that rule of thumb did not apply to us. I was happy to create something that worked for my children, even though it might not be what the experts recommend in books about divorce.

I learned how important it was to listen to my own guidance. For me, trusting my own feelings took a lot of practice.

I was still trying to please everyone and be the perfect human being. I was trying to do it all the right way. Allowing my children NOT to visit their father was a huge step in connecting with myself and trusting that when it felt right it was the right thing to do.

Wisdom from within:

We all have our own internal guidance system. We all have our own version of right and wrong. Each of us puts more value on certain areas over others.

Allow yourself to have your own version. Embrace your uniqueness.

- Breathe.
- Close your eyes.
- Imagine you are a gorgeous flower among many flowers.
- As you look around you see that each flower is distinct, no two are alike.
- You also feel that each flower is very happy to be its own flower and that there is no competition.
- Breathe in deeply and embrace your uniqueness.
- Breathe your self-love into every cell of your body.
- When you are ready, come back to the here and now and carry that acceptance of your special flower form with you along your path.

It is OK to be unique.

♥

TAXES

Was it easy to separate your financial accounts?

You know, Toni and I had a joint account well into our separation, which worked well for us. When he canceled my access to our joint account and I had to start with my separate account, it felt good.

I felt I was finally the master of my own universe. I could handle money and I was no longer so dependent on him.

When we had a joint account, I handed over the bills and he paid them… most of them, anyway. Sometimes, however, he chose which ones to pay and which to ignore and I felt very much controlled by him.

Yes, I could go shopping to buy things that the family needed and had a sort of a freedom; however, I always felt he watched over what I spent money on.

So, when he all of a sudden canceled my access to our joint account in July 2010, I was thrilled to start my own life for real now. He transferred child support and alimony to my account and I could be my very own Finance Minister. I was Chief Financial Officer of my own life now and this felt so very liberating, mature, and powerful. I could do what I wanted with the money I had, and I was not limited to what he deemed was worthy. I could put aside the money for school and taxes each month. I felt savvy.

Being your own boss is always great and I highly recommend it; however, this change came at a huge disadvantage to me.

Taxes in my country are not deducted from your salary like in other countries. Taxes are later billed to you for you to settle as a whole, meaning you pay taxes for the past year in spring of the next year and sometimes even later.

So, when I received my bill of taxes for 2009 I sent it to Toni. We still had our joint account during that period and, obviously, this was a bill he should have paid especially as he had chosen NOT to pay the bills for the children and I during our joint account time.

He sent it back and told me that if I wanted to have separate tax accounts, I had to pay it. He totally overlooked the fact that he was the one asking for split tax accounts, as it would save us money overall. Yes, I was naïve, and I trusted him to play fair!

I tried to explain to him that I could not pay the bill, as I never had that money to begin with. He just laughed and told me that he didn't have the money either.

So here I sat with bills for taxes for the years of 2009 and 2010 with no money to pay them. Remember, I only received money in my own account from August 2010 on. So, I never had the option of putting something away each month in 2009 and a good part of 2010.

There was no way I could get around paying the bills. Legally, I was responsible for my own tax bill, joint account or not. As I no longer had access to the joint account, I somehow needed to settle the debt on my own. It was a lot of outstanding money and my happiness about having separate accounts faded quickly. I was devastated.

How could he do this to me? It was obvious that I would pay taxes from August 2010 on; however, I had no means to do so for the previous years.

It really sunk in, how much Toni was only looking out for himself. He was happily spending money on luxuries and not deeming it necessary to be honorable towards the mother of his three children.

There was nothing I could do legally and so I eventually called the tax office, explaining the situation, and asking what I could do. They told me I could pay back my taxes in installments, so I started to pay back my taxes bit by bit. I was also burdened with paying the part of the taxes that would have been his share.

During that time, I got phone calls from luxury boutiques, letting me know that the things that were ordered had arrived and were ready to pick up. They still had my mobile phone number in their database, so I got the calls for Toni's new things and for the jewelry he ordered for Jane. This made me doubly furious, because apparently, he had enough money to buy things at high-end boutiques for himself and also for Jane, while I struggled to pay taxes he should have paid long ago!

The audacity of it all took my breath away. I shared about the phone calls from high-end luxury boutiques with friends and they told me to go pick the packages up myself; however, I was not that strong or cheeky, though now I think it would have been fun, wouldn't it?

I still get angry when I think about how unfair it was, and how little he listened to reason. How could he expect me to pay 19 months of taxes on my own, when I did not even have the money for it in the first place? I still remember his smug face, the victorious smile he sneered at me. Was this truly the man I felt I loved all those years?

I know I should not have been as trusting. I should have been more on top of things. I should have made sure he paid our taxes while we still had the joint account. I was stupid and never realized how calculating he could be.

He was always nice to me when we were together, but I saw his temper and nastiness when he dealt with waiters or people at the check-in counter. I always excused it as him being stressed. Now I saw clearly that he was just a nasty person and his nastiness had been turned towards me. I finally saw his true face. He even had a smirk on his face, seeing me devastated and suffocating under tax bills.

I survived that battle and I am deeply proud of myself. I managed to balance my budget despite the huge tax debts I had, and I am paying my taxes on time each time now. I put aside the necessary amount every month so I have the total saved by spring of the following year. I am a good financial manager and that is something I am extremely proud of. Never again do I want to have the feeling of not being able to pay my bills, no matter what they are. I am glad I got my separate account, at a different bank as well, completely separate from Toni. I am now financially free and independent of my ex and it feels great.

In hindsight, one is always cleverer; however, this was such a valuable lesson for me. Despite the fact that I was nearly drowning in tax debt, I made it out alive and the feeling I got afterward is something that I just wouldn't miss for the world.

I can do it *myself*, despite all the odds. I am able to handle anything Toni throws at me.

Wisdom from within:

When I feel overwhelmed, I usually take a walk in nature. This frees my mind and I feel so much more at peace.

While walking and looking around at the beauty around me, I can let go of my worries. I arrive in the here and now, and feel supported. Trust that everything will be all right eventually bubbles up and I can carry this into my daily life.

Breathing in, taking fortifying breaths, and then letting all of the stress and frustration go as I exhale through my open mouth, releasing and healing.

Nature is our great healer and is readily available to mostly all of us. If you live in a city, you can go to a park or even find a tree to admire near you.

♥

CHIPS ON THE FLOOR

Did you ever question the parenting abilities of your ex?

Oh yes, there were many times when I realized Toni probably wouldn't be nominated for Parent of The Year. When we were together, it didn't matter. I was there to keep them showered with love. Whenever the kids came back from a weekend with their dad's, however, there was always some incident that happened during their visit.

One Sunday evening was especially hard. All three came home looking like they had gone through a storm. They were very unsettled, and it took me a while to get to the bottom of things. As usual, I did not want to probe. It felt like they were just more 'off' than usual. I didn't want to jump to conclusions because it was possible that nothing major had happened. When they finally opened up and shared how unsettling it had been at their dad's, I was shocked.

It was only natural that my kids would not feel at ease at their dad's, especially after Jane moved in with her two girls. It was only normal that my kids acted up because they did not feel comfortable, because they were not given attention, because they felt left out, because there was no one looking after them, and mostly because they lacked emotional support.

In this particular incident, they were eating chips before dinner and the bowl was empty, so Catherine asked for more. Apparently, she did not ask politely enough and probably did not say please, either.

Jane filled the bowl and brought it to the children, and then she threw it at Catherine. From what Catherine and they boys said, she actually *threw* the bowl with chips at my daughter!

She started tearing into Catherine, telling her how naughty and misbehaved she was. Jane probably complained to Toni, who was cooking in the kitchen (the area was open).

My children were astonished, not that I never screamed at them; however, throwing a bowl full of food at them was a bit over the top. First of all, these were not her kids, and secondly she could have hurt Catherine.

If this wasn't bad enough, when Toni was serving dinner, he called everyone to the table except for Catherine.

He told her to clean up the chips before she could sit down to eat.

Catherine was astonished, so was I when I heard about it. It was not like the bowl had fallen to the ground by Catherine's hand. It was not an accident either. No, Jane deliberately threw the bowl and then Catherine had to pick up the mess?

What kind of message was this, I wondered? Adults can behave any way they want, as long as they make the kids clear up the mess? Blame a young girl for anything you want?

Yes, she might have been naughty, but she did not throw the bowl nor dump the chips on the floor – and she certainly did not deserve to have a bowl thrown at her. All children can be naughty from time to time, especially when dealing with a new family situation and the discomfort it causes. Jane might have tried being the adult and reminding Catherine of her manners instead of throwing something at her.

Instead, little Catherine, who was nine years old at the time, had to clear up after her stepmom's temper tantrum while all the others were starting dinner at the table. I am not sure she ever joined them for dinner that evening because she was just so stunned, humiliated, and ashamed.

After hearing that story, I felt like Catherine was in her very own Cinderella story with a wicked stepmother. In addition, Catherine's dad was immature, in my opinion anyway, one who didn't even bother to protect his own children or step up in their defense. What is worse, having a father who is not here for you, or a father who is gone? Remember, too, Catherine had been his little princess before the separation, so this stung just a bit more for her.

That evening, I truly wondered what was going on at their dad's place and whether my children would ever feel safe there.

I talked to all three of my kids, letting them know that sometimes life treats us unfairly. I explained that if someone (even your dad) blames you for something, it doesn't mean you were to blame. Even dads can be wrong.

Holding my children in love, reassuring them that I would always be there for them was my most important role in this time of need. I apologized to them for them being unfairly treated. I hugged them; sharing love and understanding, and I encouraged them to speak up for themselves and also to speak up for each other. I told them that they always had each other, that together they could be stronger especially during the times I was not with them.

For me it was a huge challenge to let my kids go and visit their dad after that, knowing what a harsh atmosphere they found there. I always thought other moms would be similar to me or at least nurturing; however, I found out that some moms are different, and unfortunately Toni picked one of those different moms.

Letting my kids find their way through it all, trusting and sending them love while they were away, keeping them in safe and beautiful thoughts and energy was all I could do when they visited their father. It was kind of like their early teenage years when I had to learn to let go, trust, share safety measures, and encourage them to speak up, even if it was hard.

There was a lesson for them in this as well as one for me. It is not like we have to accept everything that comes our way. It is not OK to be blamed and treated badly by anyone, and especially not by a stepmom.

Breathing – taking deep full belly breaths – has helped me stay calm and centered. When I am centered and calm, my children can find their calm too (perhaps Jane could have learned this technique and applied it in her own life). Learning to stay calm and simply listening to them, embracing them, loving them was the hardest part.

I often wanted to storm out and drive to their dad's and knock some sense into him and yes, I honestly wanted to kick his girlfriend. I knew, however, deep down inside I knew that would upset my children even more. What they needed was for me to stay calm and reassuring and to just hold them, so they could let go of this situation and the experience. A beautiful trusting atmosphere took hold of the four of us as a result of these incidents, and it bonded us even closer together.

Wisdom from within:

All we need is love and love is all we need, just like The Beatles said.

No matter how hard any situation is, there is always time to come back to our hearts and our inner center.

- Rub your hands together until they are warm.
- Put one hand on your forehead and the other on your heart area. This will bring a calm atmosphere back to you.
- Keep on breathing in and out. Breathe in through your nose and out through your mouth.
- Maybe shake your body in order to shake the bad feelings, energy, and stress off.

Do this as long and as often as you need to.

♥

SUMMER BREAK

How did you feel about letting your children visit your ex after all of this?

You know, as a full-time mom, all I ever wanted was a bit of peace and quiet. I imagined taking a weekend away from it all to recharge. When Toni and I split up, I had every other weekend off all of a sudden. This felt really odd, not at all like what I thought I wanted. Be wary of what you wish for!

Of course, it was especially hard for me to relax after I learned that the kids never felt good or comfortable at their dad's house – that made me stress out the whole time they were away instead of giving me the mental space to unwind.

So, the first summer after our separation, Toni wanted to take the kids for a 10-day vacation. It felt really weird for the kids to be gone for so long and I was so lonely at that time, even though I made plans with friends and kept myself busy for the majority of the time.

Originally, he wanted to be away on my birthday and I said, "No. I do NOT want to celebrate my birthday without my children". It just didn't feel right. Luckily, he was cooperative for once and planned on having the kids back by my birthday.

Just to give you a little information: during the two summers we were separated, Toni and Jane had taken all five kids (her two and my three) to a resort. They left the five children unsupervised at the pool while they went to the gym or spa during the day. This was an absolutely unacceptable situation in my mind, as Horatio was only five years old and was not fully able to swim at the time. I saw all the danger my ex put the kids in and, before they went the following year, I asked the older children to look after Horatio even though it was not really their duty. Their dad wouldn't supervise the children and I'd rather have Mathew and Catherine making sure Horatio survived the summer break.

I mean, it is OK to allow the children to be independent in my opinion; however, it is clearly an issue to put them at risk. And really - five kids alone at a hotel pool? How did other guests feel about this?

The second year, the boys were in a room with a TV and the girls were in a room without, so all the girls swarmed the boys' room at night to watch TV until well after midnight, even though both boys were tired and would have preferred to sleep.

The adults didn't seem to be present for the children at night either. After they had their nightcap at the bar, they said goodnight to the kids and went off to their room, leaving the kids to tend to themselves. There was no bedtime and no rules after hours.

Horatio came home from that trip exhausted and aggressive; he needed to let off steam. It disturbed him very much to have the girls sitting on his bed, watching TV, when he actually just wanted to sleep. He was younger than all the others and ended up being very tired as he never got any real rest at night and the kids were constantly on the go during the day, too. It was just too much for him.

I know I need time out just to relax and unwind. We all need a break from the commotion every now and then – especially children. We need time to recharge, time to enjoy the quiet and just be, without too much going on. Constant noise and action are not good for anyone, especially not young children who are swimming and playing all day and then staying up until midnight or later.

For me, those summer breaks when the kids were away with their dad were hard. Yes, I enjoyed my time by myself; however, getting them ready was stressful and afterward, having them come home completely off kilter, was very strange. They needed a vacation after their vacation.

When they came home from trips with Toni, I found things in their bags that did not belong to them and I was never sure if they brought back all their stuff, which was OK and again, I always involved them in packing because I felt it was important that they learn to be responsible for their own things. They went on school trips, too, where there is no mother around packing up after them. However, during school trips, they were better supervised. Funny how I trusted the teachers and chaperones with my children more than I trusted my own ex-husband.

Let's get back to the story. They had to drive the six-hour trip to the hotel in two cars and there was an incident where Catherine was kicked out of one car and had to ride in the other, but she could not tell me why when I asked her about it later on. She was very disturbed about it though.

It was hard letting them go and it was really hard knowing that they were having experiences I would rather have prevented in the first place. Looking back, I know we all learned so much from these trips: letting go, trusting the process, and knowing my kids would be alright, plus taking the extra precaution of asking the older ones to look after Horatio when they were at the pool.

My kids didn't go on any other vacations with Toni after that last trip. I think the whole thing was too stressful for them and again, it was not really about being with their dad. The adults kind of just let the children play together and while they did their own thing.

I know there are other fathers out there who take their kids on vacations and even make a point to spend time with their kids so that they have extra bonding time. Toni is not one of those dads. It saddens me, and I have apologized to my kids for this many times. I feel it is important for them to get to know their father as he is, though. They know that their relationship with him could be different and that other fathers do things differently, as they often hear from their friends.

For me, it is important to let my kids know that the way their dad treats them is not about them but about their dad. There is nothing they, as children, did wrong or even could do wrong. It is a parenting failure on his part.

I wish they could have a good time at their dad's house and want to see him. I wish I could know they were safe and happy in his care.

When they were with him, I found time to do extra things for myself. One time, I spent a week at an energy course with beautiful friends, learning how to feel more energetic and how to look after myself as a healer, especially while being around other people. This was the first time I spent some time alone doing something that I was interested in. I had a wonderful time and developed a better sense of myself during the course. When I had the free time, I was able to connect more deeply with myself, which was something I was unable to really do while looking after three kids, getting them to school, and taking care of a home and household. Having the time to ask myself what I would love to do was refreshing. Allowing myself to do what I loved to do and having the freedom was pure bliss.

Making the best out of each situation is important – and that's what we tried to do with regard to vacations with their father. All I could really do was send them love, wish them a great time with their dad and stepfamily, and allow myself to make plans to do something that I enjoyed. This time helped me deeply on my path to reconnect with Caroline. I could be Caroline for a little bit when they were away before I went back to being Mom when they returned home.

Wisdom from within:

We can always ask the Universe to look after our loved ones, so that we feel like we do our share without actually being there. Sometimes asking the Universe for help is all we can do, and this has to be good enough.

You can speak to the Universe like you would with a friend, or you can choose to have a conversation with the Universe in your mind.

Some simple rules:

Word your request in a positive manner, as the Universe doesn't hear the words no and *not*. For example, it is better to say, "Make sure my kids are safe," instead of, "Please do not let anything happen to them."

Handing your burdens and worries off to the Universe can help you to be more relaxed.

If you worry constantly, you are actually sending that distressed wish to the Universe. That's why you want to keep your thoughts positive.

Imagine your kids having fun, being safe, and having a great time.

♥

HORATIO DOESN'T WANT TO GO

Was there a moment when you felt like the most horrible mom ever?

I mean, I never felt good enough and often had moments where I felt I should have done this or that better. Mostly, I felt I should have had more patience with my kids, especially when they were younger. I did not like noise and that was not always easy to deal with because I had two boisterous boys in my home.

I always had deep empathy for my children, though, and sometimes it was hard leaving them at Kindergarten or school when they were crying.

I still remember one time when Horatio did not want to visit his dad and cried so hard about having to go. I can still feel it in my bones, so to speak. I hoped he would be fine, like kids usually are a minute after you drop them off at school. This story, however, still tears at my heart.

It's no wonder I kept this chapter to be the last to write. It took me courage to express this openly, as it truly makes me feel like the worst mom on earth. How could I have done this to him? Why didn't I give in to Horatio, like every cell in my body screamed for me to do? There is still the lingering guilt and the question, was I too selfish?

I know life comes with a learning curve. This one was steep though!

It was late summer or early autumn in the first year of our separation. Toni was due to pick up the kids for their weekend at his place. Horatio did *not* want to go. He clung to me. When Toni rang the doorbell the other two got into the car with their little overnight bags; however, Horatio wouldn't let me go.

I looked at Toni for help. I hoped he could entice Horatio to come to him.

All he said like he wanted to be on his way – presto – was, "He has to want to come!"

For me, it felt like a blow to the stomach. It was like the king was offering his time and little Horatio was not valuing it. I was devastated; I wondered why Toni couldn't act like he cared just once? Why couldn't he show any sort of patience, like a teacher who fully understands that things sometimes take a while to get used to? Horatio was about six years old, still very young, and it would take time and patience to help him to adjust to the new situation. Sometimes all he wanted was Mommy and that was both OK and totally normal.

Then Toni said, "Jane is looking forward to seeing you."

My mind sputtered: What, why, how? Wait a minute! Weren't the kids there to see their dad? Why on earth could he mention that his girlfriend wants to see Horatio? It did not make sense.

Didn't *he* want to see his kids? Why couldn't he say *he* was looking forward to spending time with his son? Or something along the lines of, "We are going do this or that and we have a great time." Would that have been so hard?

Horatio was still clinging to me and he could hang on tight! It felt like he was holding on for his life. He probably was, but I chose to ignore it, though. I didn't really feel like I had a choice.

Toni got fed up and went into the car, starting the engine and demanding that I get Horatio into the car.

So much for thinking he would help. Did I truly need another reminder that he was not the most caring father? He certainly gave me one that day.

So, I carried little Horatio to the car. I sat him in his car seat as gently as I could and then I buckled him in. I tried to remove his arms from around my neck. All the while, he was sobbing and crying and breaking my heart. I tried to close the car door; however, his arms came out and I did not want to shut his finger or arm in the car door. I tried to fold his arms in and close the door while holding back my tears.

"Am I doing the right thing?" I kept asking myself over and over. My instinct was to grab Horatio and take him back into the house to cuddle and soothe him for the rest of the weekend. But I felt that he might calm down after he was at his dad's place like he would do after I left him in the classroom at school.

All evening, I was waiting for a text from Toni, letting me know that Horatio was OK. It never came. I was so nervous and worked up, so I finally grabbed my phone and texted him. "How is Horatio?" I asked. He texted back that all was fine.

At last, I felt like I could relax and feel more at ease. Folding a crying and clingy child into his dad's car was more than I could handle on the best of days.

When all three came home on Sunday evening, Horatio was so quiet and tired. I hugged him and cuddled him. I was so happy to have my three back home.

I asked, "How was it? Did you have fun?"

Then the older kids told me that Horatio had been crying ALL weekend long.

It hit me. I felt my stomach drop. I had no idea. Why did Toni lie to me? Why didn't he call me? I would have picked Horatio up in the blink of an eye. All I ever wanted was for my kids to be fine.

Horatio was obviously not fine, and this was much more serious than him crying for a minute when I dropped him off at school.

Guilt washed over me. Why had I not listened to my inner voice? Why was I so determined to see him off to visit his dad? Was having some time to myself more important than the wellbeing of my child?

It took me a long while to calm down. I comforted myself with the knowledge that my three kids were back home and fine.

I allowed Horatio to lie in my bed and cuddle with me, reestablishing trust and a sense of wellbeing. I allowed him to hug me as often as he wanted (I always did that anyway; however, this time I made extra sure he got the comfort he so needed).

After a couple of days pondering, I realized that I had not handed Horatio over so that I could enjoy a peaceful weekend by myself. No. I sent him with his dad with the belief that he needed to see his father regularly, as stated in the books I read about going through a divorce and children's wellbeing.

I expected Toni to be more like an understanding teacher and caregiver. I never realized how overwhelmed and clueless he could feel with a crying child, nor was I fully aware that he did not want to look like a failure. He would NEVER admit that Horatio did not stop crying, so he lied to me, just so he could look better.

Also, his words, "He has to want to come!" when he picked Horatio up haunted me. Yes, as parents, we want our children to sprint into our arms. It is natural for children to feel happy to see their parents; however, some parent-child relationships are different.

It should have been a clue for me that Horatio was vehemently opposed to going to visit his dad.

It was the first and the last time I forced one of my children to see their dad. It was a painful lesson, one I took to heart never to repeat again.

Maybe I needed this wake-up call to accept our different circumstances. I had to accept the fact that Toni was not like the regular dads described in all of those books. I realized that, if a little boy does not want to go to visit his father, he has his reasons. Children are human beings and often know better than adults give them credit for.

I also learned to do it my way, the way that I felt best served my kids and catered to their wellbeing.

Yes, I still feel a bit guilty for feeling like I forced my gentle-hearted boy to go to visit his dad when he so desperately did not want to go. Even if my intentions were good, it was definitely not the right thing to do. I learned the hard way.

We always know better afterward. Hindsight is 20/20. I've learned to trust my instincts more and how to say NO.

Accepting our situation as unique and making the necessary adjustments to deal with it all was one big learning step. It was something I had to allow myself to do, too. I had to learn to pay more attention to what my heart said than what books said, as books only give general advice but not advice about special cases, like ours.

Wisdom from within:

It is OK to give in. It is very much OK to do things differently.

If you ask ten people the same question, you get ten different opinions. There is never just a right or a wrong way. It is never as simple as black or white. Allow yourself to go into the grey zones, or, even better, into the rainbow-colored zones.

I always love to Ask Archangel Michael to help me cut energetic cords.

- Sit comfortably
- Breathe in and out, taking deep belly breaths
- Close your eyes
- Ask Archangel Michael to come to you
- Ask Archangel Michael to cut all the cords around you
- Imagine him taking his mighty sword and swishing around you, cutting all the cords to all the negative energies
- Allow him to take his time
- Ask him to cut all the cords to guilt, worries, fear, pain and hurt
- Breathe in and out
- Let it all go
- Maybe you feel a tingling, maybe you feel refreshed, just take it as it comes.
- Thank Archangel Michael, and ask him to always protect you

I love this exercise; it always gives me a fresh start. I sometimes love to do this in the evenings too, before I go to bed, so I have a more peaceful night.

♥

IT IS HER LOSS

Are father-daughter relationships special in your mind?

Oh yes, there can be a very special bond between a father and a daughter. I know Catherine adored her father, he was her knight in shining armor and she was his princess.

It was devastating for her when her father left, especially since she lost her place as his princess in the process. Somehow, that special bond was severed without her doing anything wrong. It was especially hard for me to observe.

Still, I feel she grew into the amazing young woman she is today in spite of it all, or maybe because she had to find her own way and could not rely on being the princess any longer.

I treasured how much closer Catherine and I got during the whole break up.

I treasure the bonds I have with each one of my children, honestly, and am proud of all three of them. They are special and so unique. I am proud to call them my children.

But, as you know, Catherine suffered immensely under the separation and it was especially hard for her, which does not mean it was not hard for the boys, too. It just felt to me like she had something of a harder fall than the boys did because of her special relationship with her father.

The first year after Toni and I split up, the children saw their dad more or less regularly, and then, as time went on, less and less so.

One day, a while after we had separated, Toni called our house phone to wish Catherine a happy birthday. I picked it up and walked upstairs to hand over the phone to Catherine. She stood there like a deer in the headlights, fearful and shocked, and just shook her head. I held my hand over the phone and told her it was her dad. She said she did not want to talk to him.

I accepted this. I put the phone back to my ear and told Toni that Catherine did not want to come to the phone.

All he said was, "Weird."

I waited for him to say something more, maybe even ask me why she didn't want to talk. He just let me go.

I wanted to share why she didn't want to talk with him, as I could see and sense what was going on. She felt neglected, betrayed, and emotionally distant from Toni after all that they had gone through with him and Jane; however, I waited for him to ask me to explain. I knew if I shared this wisdom without being asked, he would not have been able to take it. He was not ready to hear it. If he would have asked me, I would have been willing to share my insights. Of course, he did not ask.

Toni always acted as none of the issues he was facing with the kids was his fault. It must be her, of course. She must be having a bad day or maybe her mother was influencing her against her own father. Yes, that must be it. It would be so much easier for him to blame others than to have to face the truth. It seemed to me that he wasn't capable of finding fault or taking any blame for the way his relationships with the kids were going – he deflected blame to everyone else.

I was not surprised when I heard that he felt it was my fault, yet again.

However, I was shocked when I later heard he told the boys that it was her loss.

He actually sat there and said to them, "It is Catherine's loss!"

How could it be her loss? What was her loss? Dealing with an emotionally absent father? How could he be so obnoxious?

Catherine heard her brothers telling me this and looked at me with big, sad eyes. I took her in my arms and told her, "If you did not want to speak to me anymore, I would be devastated. I would be so sad and it would be absolutely MY LOSS. I would come and try to find out what happened and what I could do to make things better between us".

She smiled at me with tears in her eyes. I told her how proud I was of her and how truly wonderful she is in my eyes.

I felt I needed to protect her from the cold behavior of her father. How could he hurt his little girl's heart so much?

It was no excuse that he did not even realize the effect his words and actions had, or that he could rationalize it in his own mind any way he liked. It was his fault and absolutely *his loss*, having no relationship with his own flesh and blood, his one and only daughter.

How could it be her loss? I felt she had not lost much, anyway. Whether she was on speaking terms with her absent father or not, there was not so much of a difference, is there?

What did I learn from this experience? I learned to keep my mouth shut. Yeah, I remembered not to give my two cents to Toni, I knew he would not take it anyway. He preferred to blame and divert. Still, I had hoped he would want to reach out and maybe ask me for my advice, as the sensitive mother I am, as the person who knew our children best. I knew, however, he'd rather listen to the unsolicited advice of Jane regarding Catherine's faults.

So be it. It was (and is) his loss. I also learned that there was nothing I could do to change this; it was a hard lesson for me, as I want my children to be happy and would have done anything to salvage their relationships with their dad. It always takes two to have a relationship, and it seemingly was not meant to be for Toni and Catherine or her brothers. There is hope for the future though – there is always hope.

I once told him that the door is always open to his kids, but that HE is the adult and he has to walk through it and reach out to his children.

Wisdom from within:

Taking a step back and not reacting is one of the hardest things to do, especially if you are someone who loves to help others.

Ask the Universe for help when you need strength to remain outside of something. Ask your Universal Helpers to assist you. Hand it all over. Trust that the Universe will take care of things, and know that sometimes, it is not meant to be.

It's good to understand that the involved parties often need to learn a lesson from their own experiences, and we can't take the experiences away from anyone.

Trust and breathe, knowing that all is meant to be just the way it is, no matter how hard it feels to do so.

Breathe deeply, ask the Universe for help, and send love to all of the people involved, yourself included.

Then give yourself a pat on your back for allowing others to have their experiences as you watched on the sidelines. You did so well!

HE ALWAYS COOKS WELL

Was it hard for the kids to adjust to the separation and new family dynamics?

Oh yes, it was very hard indeed. I mean, people need time to adjust to any new situation. The kids were doing pretty good during the first couple of months of our breakup, when their dad was visiting them at our house and then when they visited him at his home. Really, everything seemed to go well until Jane moved into Toni's house with her two daughters.

That was just too much for my three. They are really very sensitive, just like me.

They felt OK visiting their dad when he still lived on his own; however, once Jane moved in with her children, things changed dramatically. They were not alone with their dad any longer. It seemed that they were barely tolerated there instead of welcome.

There were two other children living permanently with their father. There was a woman who demanded their father's attention, especially when his children were visiting.

Somehow, it felt to me like Jane was acting in a play: she wanted to make sure Toni was paying more attention to her than his own kids. Of course, it seemed he fell for it.

Maybe he was afraid of losing her? Maybe he was the giver in their relationship?

Anyway, this act was not much fun for my children and I fully understood when it was just too much for them and they did not want to go see him anymore. Some of the stories that they told me about what happened when they visited their father seemed bizarre; however, they are sadly true.

Like, one time, Catherine told me that Jane asked Toni in front of my kids, "Who do you like most?" He replied, "You, of course! You are the best thing that has ever happened to me!" It seemed such a petty comment to make.

This was soon after she moved in and I feel like she just wanted to mark her territory and especially estrange him from his daughter, who she might have seen as competition for Toni's attention. It was really silly for an adult to act like that and it was so deeply hurtful to my children, especially Catherine.

Catherine woke up one day in her worst nightmare. She was downgraded to simply some girl; Daddy had a new woman plus two new daughters in his life who he acted like they were more important to him than Catherine was.

So often she asked me, "Why does he do this or that with them and not with me?" I had no answer for her heartbreaking questions. I could not fathom why he acted like he no longer loved her. Why she, all of a sudden, was like someone else's kid to him. I still don't know how he even could seemingly turn so cold toward Catherine and my boys so quickly.

It took me a long time to comfort Catherine. I held her in her pain. I know her heart broke then and there – somehow her relationship with her father had been irreparably damaged.

Nowadays, she is not on speaking terms with him. She no longer wants him to be part of her life. I fully understand and support this. Toni still thinks he has done nothing wrong. To this day, he says he has no idea why she does not want to see him. Truly?

Another time, Mathew came home from a weekend visit at his dad's pretty down. He was normally in a good mood when he came home, as he usually hid behind his computer for most of his visit, which wasn't ideal; however, I understood his need for quiet and being out of the way.

Apparently, he had congratulated his dad on a meal he cooked. He mentioned something like, "This tastes great! Thanks, Dad, you cooked well!" Then Jane's daughter snapped, "He always cooks well for us!"

This small comment, of course, brought home the fact that Mathew's dad did not cook for him anymore. His dad was now cooking for a new family.

Mathew was very saddened, and I felt that time it really sank in, that his dad wasn't going to come back home and seemed happier with this new family.

There were so many changes for my children to deal with. It wasn't just that their dad was giving more attention to Jane and her girls, but the fact that he wasn't really giving them any attention at all when they were there to visit him.

From what I heard from the kids, it seemed like they weren't really parented when they were visiting at Toni's house. The kids told me that Toni and Jane let the kids do whatever they wanted. They were hardly ever supervised, and there wasn't a bedtime. My three were up till well after midnight on both Friday and Saturday night. It was no wonder they were always exhausted when they came back. The lack of weekend bedtime rules led to them having a hard time getting up and concentrating in school after a weekend at their dad's.

But Toni and Jane had their strict *"naptime"* every day and the kids told me that they were not to bother them until their adult nap was over.

Also, the kids told me that Jane played with food, something I strongly oppose. I have always felt that we should respect food and treat it as such and not waste it by playing with it.

One day, Jane played baseball in the kitchen with Toni, a cucumber was her bat. Of course, they had to throw the cucumber away afterward, which was a waste and not something I wanted my kids to learn.

I had to learn to accept that they had their rules and I had mine. It was hard for me to reconcile because Toni and I had previously agreed on many rules for the kids. Jane moved in and, all of a sudden, everything was different.

For me, it was extra stressful that Jane and her two daughters seemed to give my three such a hard time. I still wish Toni could have found a woman who would have been willing to integrate his children into the new family dynamic instead of competing with them.

It was not meant to be. It was hard for my three children and so it was hard for me, too.

We learned so much during this time of adjustment. We learned to depend on ourselves and, as hard as those times were, the kids saw their dad for what he was and not for what he could have been.

He was never really involved with the children when we were together, preferring to leave me with the lion's share of childcare responsibility. Even when he was still at home with us, they hardly saw him. Now he was gone, and he seemed to have a happy family of his own, one that didn't really seem to include my kids.

I was there for them and I made an extra effort to share with them that kindness is essential. I opened their eyes to all the kind people out there and also the fact that we can always help someone in need, give someone a warm smile, or take some extra caution with our words before speaking.

I love my kids dearly, no matter how their father acted or how they felt or feel about their father.

For me, accepting the fact that he was gone was much less difficult when he behaved this way. Sometimes anger helps us get over heartache, and he made it so easy for me to be angry with him because I felt that I had to fight for my children and their emotional wellbeing.

Thanks to him for being such an idiot in my eyes! I was able to step up and be more myself again, which allowed me to be an even better mother to my own children.

Wisdom from within:

It is important we allow ourselves to experience all the feelings we have. Pushing away anger, sorrow, and/or pain is not helpful. The feelings just come up over and over, until we acknowledge them.

What helps me is to sit with my feelings, acknowledge them and have a bit of a conversation with them.

- Sit somewhere comfortably
- Close your eyes
- Take some deep breaths into your belly
- Take a minute to connect with your body and feelings
- Listen within. What feelings come up?
- Ask each feeling,
- What it is you want to tell me?
- What do you need to know right now?
- What might this relate to?
- Thank your feelings - yes all of them! Tell them something like, "Thank you for showing up. Thank you for teaching me all about it."
- Take another deep breath
- Come back into the here and now

When we acknowledge our feelings, we can also set them free.

Anytime I feel a "bad" emotion, I remember to allow it and to sit with it, be it guilt, envy, or fear.

If you take time to sit with every feeling and acknowledge it, you will feel much freer than you would if you stuff them down, declaring them as unwanted, not good, or harmful.

There is also shadow work you might do, for example with the feeling of envy. While it is OK to feel envious, you can see it is a pointer showing you what you would love to have in your life as well.

♥

DAD'S KIND OF CHRISTMAS LUNCH

Do you have any particular stories that remind you of Christmas time?

The holiday season is always challenging, especially when you go through a divorce. I did not want to celebrate Christmas without my kids, so I told Toni that he could see the kids on the 26th and celebrate with them on that day; I would have them on 24th and 25th each year. I know usually it is one year with Dad and the next with Mom; however, who wants to celebrate Christmas without their kids, especially when they would be alone on that day? We came up with this solution, which felt good as the kids could see both parents each Christmas.

However, it was not such a great idea after all, or let's say that Toni didn't treat his kids like they were special to him, yet again.

The first Christmas approached. I had a great time with my three celebrating Christmas and they were happy to go to see their dad on the 26th. He came around to pick them up mid-morning. They were having lunch with him and then coming back in the evening.

I, of course, imagined a lovely family dinner where the kids would be able to enjoy some relaxed time and be with their dad even Jane and her girls. Little did I know…

When my kids came home that evening, they were completely devastated. After they settled down, they shared the story of their day with their father. Here's what they told me:

The kids arrived at their dad's house and Toni went into the kitchen to prepare lunch.

They hung around and, of course, were excited about opening presents. Then lunch came along with a series of guests arriving to eat with them. Apparently, Jane and Toni planned a party for their friends while the kids were there.

All the adults sat at one end of the table, while the kids were seated at the other end. Toni was at one end visiting with his adult friends and his kids were at the other end of the table. This was surely not how the kids imagined a lunch with Dad.

When the kids told me, all I could do was shake my head and wonder why. Again, I felt he had topped his behaviors. How could he do this?

He had many days to invite his friends over for dinner. Really, I had nothing against having friends over; however, did it really have to be the ONE day his kids would be there to celebrate the holiday with him? The people he invited were all strangers to my kids, so it was not a really Christmassy feeling. I still wonder what he was thinking – I have a hard time believing that this was a coincidence.

How did this make the children feel? They were excited to see their dad to celebrate Christmas with him and then they are just seated at the other end of a big table of adult dinner guests as if they were a nuisance and second thought?

There were about six to eight guests, so it was not just another couple and Horatio told me one of them was a true witch. He confided, "Mom, she was so mean."

I was also wondering what happened to Toni to make him change so much. The guy I knew was hiding at his computer all the time and now he was throwing big parties with strangers? I still wonder whether they had friends over so he did not have to feel awkward being with his kids. Maybe it was all a deflection? Either way, it was pitiful to me!

Toni was so proud of the party he even sent over pictures and told me to look at how happy the kids were. I took one look at the picture and saw the pain in their eyes, the sadness, the loneliness, and the disappointment. I even showed the picture to the child psychologists and they were puzzled at his misinterpretation of their feelings. So, I was relieved that I had the backing of the psychologists. I had seen the truth, even though it was not something I wanted to see.

What an unforgettable Christmas they spent at their dad's! I wish it could have been unforgettable for the right reasons, though.

The following year, Horatio was clever! He called me at 2 pm. "Mom please pick me up. I want to come home!" I asked him whether his dad knew about this and was OK with it – he said it was OK. So, I drove there; Horatio came dashing out of the house and hopped into my car, so happy and relieved he could escape. Toni and Jane followed with a bag of presents. Jane even came and hugged me, which was really awkward; her pretending like all was well between us. She then hugged Horatio and baby talked to him as if she adored him. It was such a weird situation. Knowing how she treated the children from their stories, I saw through her. I knew it was all an act. Pretense. On their way back into the house Jane made a big show of hugging Toni while looking back at me, showing me that he was all hers now.

"You can have him," I thought, "but you'd better not treat my kids badly!"

The following year, Horatio said, "Mom, I only go for the presents." I just nodded because I knew they did not have much of their dad's attention anyway and my then seven-year-old was so clever and on point. I understood where he was coming from.

It wasn't the most fabulous Christmas time for my kids. I am not sure; in the end, they might have gone to visit Toni two or three times after that. Then they stopped going to see him or visit him, even on weekends. Nowadays, they see him every now and then for lunch or dinner in a restaurant, a neutral zone which is great and usually without Jane, which is probably even better.

I still wonder why a mostly absent parent would hold a big party on the one day his kids visit. It bothers me that Toni never felt it was important to spend time with his kids, especially when he did not see them so often. Obviously, they were not very high on his priority list, which is a pity, mostly for him, as he had no idea what he was missing out on.

What did I learn from it all? I learned that quiet time and quality time with my children was and is very important. I learned that they needed more time to adjust and also, I realized how much I valued my children and the time we had.

Even then I knew that they'd eventually grow up and I might not see them over Christmas anymore. However, I wanted to make the most of every Christmas we spent together.

Christmas is never about the presents. It is about *being* present, present with your own children. Being with my children has always been my greatest gift to me.

I also learned to go with the flow of it all. I had to accept that the kids' dad was far from perfect and I make sure to be there to hold them in love, to hug them, and be there for them. Yes, being a mom was my full-time job and something that my children needed desperately. Through all those experiences with Toni, Jane, and the kids, I learned to value myself more and to treasure the time I spent with my kids when they needed me the most.

Wisdom from within:

Be fully present and mindful.

- Sit still and connect with each one of your senses (a couple of minutes for each)
- Ask yourself the following questions:
- What are you seeing, truly seeing?
- What are you hearing, truly hearing?
- What are you feeling? (Your chair? Clothes? How do they feel on your skin?)
- What do you smell?
- What are you tasting? How does your tongue feel in your mouth?

Really concentrate on the now by connecting with one sense at a time.

Afterwards, you will feel more present, more at peace, and right here in the moment.

♥

I'LL PAY YOU ONLY WHEN WE ARE DIVORCED

Were there any scary moments for you during the divorce and separation?

Oh yes, there were many scary moments. There were the times I feared for the well-being of my kids and there were the moments I had no idea how to make ends meet.

One such moment, in particular, was when I moved into a new home about two years after our separation.

Here in my country, it is very common to rent a home. Toni and I, however, owned the house we used to live in because I wanted stability for my children as they were growing up. I did not want them to face too much upheaval during their lives.

I was not "in love" with the house we had. We chose it because his books fit into it nicely, because it was representative of our lifestyle and success, and because it had enough room. I loved it for the huge garden with mature bushes and trees that came with the house. I knew the kids would love to play there. I was just pregnant with Catherine when we bought the property. Mathew already loved to play in the garden while we were renovating the house.

It did not sell while we were abroad for Toni's work, so when we came back, it was ours to move back into – now with three kids, as Horatio was born while we were away.

I still loved the garden and yes, I made the house our home. However, driving the kids to the school every day was such a long ride. I felt like I was in the car all the time, shuttling them back and forth. Plus, all of their friends lived far away so play dates were not really convenient.

When Toni moved out, I stayed there for the first two years to maintain stability for the kids; however, I was more than ready to move into something that represented ME more.

I had been looking at places closer to the kids' school and we found a beautiful house to rent with a nice sized garden, as Horatio loved to play soccer. All four of us loved it the minute we walked in. It felt like this house had been waiting for us, it just felt so right. We were happy.

Moving was such a big task. Our old house had built in cupboards, so I needed to order a lot of new furniture, plus there was so much to go through and get rid of, moving from a huge house into a tiny house. Lifting boxes lead me to have a tennis elbow, which was not very comfortable.

I had one-month overlay, so I had enough time to move our things into our new home. Luckily, I did not have to move all in one day. The kitchen was ready when we moved in, so I was able to put away all the china and everything in advance.

We did it! We finally lived in our new place. Everything was there and mostly set up. You can surely imagine, moving is always a bit of a hassle and there was still plenty to do after you've moved, and there is still too much to find a place for. However, I was happy, relieved, and so proud of what I had achieved. I felt like I was finally living in a place, for the first time in my life, that *I chose*, that was ME. It felt so amazing; however, the joy did not last long.

A couple of days after we moved in – it was towards the end of the month, in March 2011 – I realized that Toni had not transferred the monthly child support and alimony payment we had agreed upon. So, I sent him an email, reminding him to transfer the money. I was polite because I thought he might have forgotten. Little did I know of the devilish arrogant attitude (my perception) he could have.

I was so shocked when I got his reply: "I will pay you once we are divorced." He was blackmailing me into agreeing to a swift divorce. What was so shocking about this to me was the fact that *he* was the one not responding to *us*. I was so ready to get rid of him once and for all – but he was stalling.

I sat there with tears filling my eyes. I was so shocked and still exhausted from the move, having done all of it myself. I was truly feeling the weight of the responsibility of it all, and then I was sitting in MY new home, not able to pay rent? How would this look? What would the landlord think when I was off to such a bad start?

I had just moved. We'd moved out of our old house so Toni could sell it, and this was how he thanked me for hurrying?

Having no money at all felt so scary, like I would be evicted out of the rental house and I wondered what would happen to my children. I was shaken to the core. I felt helpless, so very helpless. What could I do?

To top it off, Toni did not pay the part of his bonus we had agreed to. I had counted on using this money he promised to pay for the new furniture I needed.

He laughed at me in his email response, telling me that I had nothing in writing and he would never ever part with any bit of his money.

Back then, I still felt that he earned it and so it was his and I thought I needed to be nice to him so he would give it to me.

Now, I was sitting there with no money at all, not knowing how I would pay the rent or any other bills and I had no idea how to afford food to feed my kids.

I realized that no matter what I did, Toni would try to hold his strings over me. He could and would do as he pleased with no regards for his children. He felt that it was his money and his money, only; however, this time was when I had the first inkling of knowing that part of his money was mine, too.

I earned a part of his money by being the mother of his children. I earned it by moving from place to place for his career. I earned it by taking care of our home and children, so he could make a career. It seemed he took it all for granted, though.

I felt used by him. I felt worthless anyway after all I had been through with him and I felt totally defenseless. I felt like a punching bag; he could do whatever he liked to me and I had to take it.

I thought there was nothing I could do to force him to stick to our agreement because he never signed anything. He never wanted to, and I trusted him. I trusted his word. I trusted that he would value the fact that I was looking after his kids. In his eyes, it seemed all of my sacrifices and help I had given was not worth a dime and it also seemed like his kids did not matter too much to him either.

At that moment, I knew I had to step up. I had to learn to value myself, otherwise, no one ever would.

I discovered that I was not just a mom, I was a lioness. I was also the cook, the chauffeur, the nurse, the psychologist, the maid, and everything else in one. One thing this separation taught me was that my job was (and is) so very important. I was the only one looking after the wellbeing of my children and they needed me during the separation more than ever. The separation was a trauma for them and my duty was to hold them in love and reassure them and make sure they were well cared for. This took so much energy and so much dedication. For the sake of my children, I was (and am) worth it and I was going to stand up for myself and for us.

For the first time, I felt like I was doing my job. My job was to look after the children, to be The Mom, which was a very important job in my books.

I was stepping up and I learned that, even though he earned the money by working at the office, I earned part of it by looking after his children and home and by being by his side for 20 years. It was as simple as that!

Of course, it took me many more years to fully embrace the wonderful thought of being worthy. The seed had been planted that day when I read that he wouldn't pay a penny till we were divorced. Thank you, dear Toni. I learned so much from this incident.

You might wonder how we survived financially. Luckily, the laws here in my country are good towards full-time moms. So, a little letter from my lawyer reminding him that he had to fulfill his obligation to support his dependent wife and children was enough for him to grudgingly pay his monthly support. I never saw part of his bonus though, but I still managed to pay all my bills from the move over the following months, partially by selling things I didn't need any longer.

I was so embarrassed by the delay in making payments as I always paid my bills on time, and this time, it took me a while to pay off my debts. Still, I managed it all on my own and I was proud of the fact.

There is always a way to manage and that is wonderful. I learned that I was the only person I could trust, and that was a good starting point for the coming months and years. I learned that I could do it.

Self-worth is such an important lesson to learn. I had no self-worth at all coming out of the marriage, but enough was enough. The more Toni threw at me, the more I was ready to stand up to him and fight for my worth. Reading spiritual books, listening to my internal guidance, and connecting to my own essence helped me find my worth as well. Once I found my internal value, it was much easier to stand up for my children and myself and to make sure we got what we deserved.

Wisdom from within:

I love affirmations like:

- I am lovable
- I am worthy of love
- I am so worthy
- I am worthy just by being me
- I am enough

Saying those out loud over and over and spread over days and weeks have helped me truly feel worthier.

Also, write down one thing you are proud of yourself for each day. Keep the list for a day when you aren't feeling so confident and valuable.

♥

THREE GIRLS AT TOY STORE

Were there any mistaken identities between your children and your ex-husband's stepchildren??

This story is actually very sad.

A friend of mine mentioned that she saw Toni in a toy store with three girls just before Christmas. She said, "Oh how wonderful that he takes Catherine and her friends shopping."

I looked at my friend and told her Catherine had not been with her dad and that Toni never took Catherine to the toy store, not even when we were still together.

My friend was so apologetic and I felt so deeply sad for Catherine.

I never told Catherine that her dad went shopping with those three girls. I never wanted her to feel sad or left out.

However, I wondered why this man could do things now with Jane's kids that he never ever did with his own kids. How could he be a better dad to someone else's kids?

Also, why was he able to take a day off from work when he never had time to take a day off while we were still together?

I know he was with Jane's daughters at the toy store and they probably invited the girl living next door.

Perhaps Jane was more willing to hand over the responsibility of her children over to Toni when she was tired or wanted to do something for herself. From the way she treated my children, I couldn't see her as being a warm and concerned parent. While I hesitated to leave my children with Toni because it seemed that he just had no interest in interacting with them, she seemed happy to send hers on errands and whatnot with him. He might have wanted to prove he was a good father and was happy to step up for Jane's children in a way he never did for ours.

Oh, how I wished he would do something with his own kids. During all the time we were together, I wanted him to make time for his own kids, but work always seemed more important to him.

Maybe it was because I was such a good mom to our children; I was a Mother Hen and maybe sometimes a bit overprotective. Also, I was so used to managing everything and I never took the chance to delegate small tasks to him. I just took care of everything and when he had no time that was OK because I was used to doing everything for the kids anyway.

Maybe, maybe he felt intimidated by me. Maybe he did not want a relationship with his kids because I was such a prominent mother? Could that be?

Honestly, even if it were true, it would all be just a lame excuse. You see, I was still blaming myself for things that went wrong. I always analyzed my behavior, which was totally normal, but also detrimental. I had to learn to accept the fact that Toni wasn't a great father, at least in my eyes.

He never tried to create a loving relationship with our kids. I made sure the door was always open; all he had to do was to step through it and reach out to his own children.

Sometimes, I wished he would have taken his own three kids on a trip to the toy store. I wondered how he felt taking practical strangers. It would probably be easier if Jane's kids rejected him. It might not hurt him as much as being rejected by his own kids would.

Who was I to analyze him, anyway?

There was one birthday Catherine didn't even get a present. She told me that, when he asked what she wished for, she said she had no idea. Sometimes kids just want to be surprised or there is nothing they truly wish for. That is totally normal and OK. However, that year she didn't get anything from Toni. He told her, "No wish, no gift," and used that as an excuse for not giving her a present for her birthday that year.

To me, this was unbelievable. There are always gift certificates. There is always something you can give a child – your own daughter – even if you don't know her well enough. He could have even contacted me and asked me what she liked.

Can you believe that he just did not get her anything? I feel that, in a way, it showed me how much he truly cared for his children.

Don't get me wrong, it is not that I think the more expensive the present, the more the love is there. Not at all. However, to me it is the thought of a gift, the time spent pondering ideas, the feeling of surprising your own daughter, catching the sparkle in her eyes when she was opening this surprise gift, and really just seeing her smile. Personally, I love giving something heartfelt; something I know will be the right present for the person.

I am sure he figures out what to give Jane for her birthday and for Christmas, without her having to voice a wish!

Catherine has grown up now. Only recently, she decided to cut all connections to her dad. She hopes he doesn't come to her graduation. She is done with him.

I can see clearly why. He hurt her once too often and didn't even bother to be there for her emotional support, either.

The other day, when Catherine and I were shopping for a new handbag at a less expensive department store, Catherine confided in me: "Mom, you know Jane's daughters all run around with designer handbags." I looked at her and hugged her. I told her that I was sorry for her. She said that it is OK. However, the pain was still very present.

She used to be Daddy's Princess, the only girl in his life. What happened? How could he reject her and hurt her so deeply? Why did he allow Jane to get in between him and his daughter? Why on earth did he pay so much more attention to Jane's daughters? And why, oh why did I have to choose him to be the father of my children?

I know that we all choose our lessons well before we came to this earth. We need to experience all this for our soul's development during this lifetime. Still, it hurts. Toni has hurt Catherine and I am hurting for my little girl.

I know she is stronger for it. She is not the pampered girl she used to be, not the one sticking out her tongue at me while sitting on Daddy's lap. No, she has become an independent and strong young woman who values herself and a daughter I am so very proud of. She has become true to herself and she knows her worth, not thanks to Toni but DESPITE him, and for that, I am very grateful indeed.

No, designer handbags don't make a person happy. She knows that. But she still wonders why he buys his stepdaughters expensive things and leaves her out. Why doesn't he even bother to give her presents?

There are simply no answers to some of the questions we have, and that is OK – not really OK, but....

I learned to accept the fact that he is just the way he is. I gave up the vain hope that he would come to his senses regarding our children. I know now that the only person anyone can ever change is himself. No matter what I say or do or think, I cannot change Toni's behavior.

During the early stages of our break up, I resented picking up the pieces he left behind. I resented him for hurting my kids and for the fact that I had to be the one to solely make them feel better. Now I treasure the fact that I was the one who comforted them through it all.

I learned to embrace being a mom even more and opened up to being the true nurturing being I am. I learned to embrace myself for caring instead of resenting it. I learned that it was OK to be so very different from Toni and not to worry about the fact that I am not like him. I am who I am, and that is very much OK – I'm just what my children needed.

Wisdom from within:

I love Ho'oponopono, the Hawaiian forgiveness ritual.

I especially use it on myself, forgiving myself for allowing others to treat me a certain way.

I stand in front of a mirror and look into my eyes, while repeating the following four short sentences over and over:

- I apologize/I'm sorry.
- Please forgive me.
- I love you.
- Thank you.

Of course, you can also use this process to forgive others.

♥

PASSPORT RENEWALS

Were there any funny stories?

There aren't that many funny stories when you go through a divorce. Of course, in retrospect, some of the stories seem funny, at least for an outside observer. So, I'd love to share the one about getting renewed passports for my children.

Here in the country where we live, each person needs a passport, as we often travel to other countries.

Our passports need to be renewed every 10 years for adults and every five years for children. The passports of my three children were expiring while my divorce was in the process of being settled, and the kids were going on school trips abroad soon after, so I needed to get their passports renewed.

It is generally an easy and straightforward process. You apply for a timeslot at the passport office online, you go there at the appointed time with your children, they take photographs and fingerprints (nowadays) right there, and you're all set. Within 10 days, you receive your brand-new passports via postal mail.

Being a well-organized mom, I made our appointments to renew the kids' passports in time in order to have them ready for my children when they needed them.

I booked a time for all three of the children to go in one day, and I also sent an email to the school to excuse the kids for the day, as we had to travel to the passport office.

Everything was organized – we were all set, or so I thought until I got a notice from the passport office that I also needed the signature of their father, as we were not yet divorced and custody was not settled.

No problem, I thought. I filled out the forms and sent them over to Toni for him to sign.

Again, I ended up being shocked by what he was capable of doing.

I got an email from him informing me that he would only sign the papers when we were finally divorced.

I remember sitting there in front of my computer, staring at the screen, rereading this email, stunned, my mouth was probably open in disbelieving shock.

"What... why... what...??" I kept stammering.

I could not, using the best of my imagination, see a connection between our divorce and a passport renewal for our kids.

I was so stunned, but then I burst out laughing.

Was he truly trying to blackmail me?

It's not that I was delaying things. I was ready to divorce him; it simply took longer than either of us expected. Part of the holdup, too, was his lawyer's turn-around time for emails and general advice.

Why blame me for all of it? Why even try to blackmail me in the first place? What about asking me? What about any normal and decent behavior? There were about 1,000 options out there for resolving this, so why on earth bring the kids into it?

I sat there for a while, focusing on breathing.

I took solace in re-organizing everything for the children. First, I wrote the school to let them know the kids wouldn't be missing school on the day I had originally arranged, as there was a delay in the appointment.

Then I soothed the kids, who were afraid they would not be able to go on their school trips. I spent the afternoon wiping their tears, hugging them, reassuring them they had done nothing wrong. I told them there was still plenty of time and that things would work out, even though, in my mind, I realized that we were probably dealing with a man who had zero scruples. I mean, was there any other excuse for his behavior?

I contacted the passport office, checked with my lawyer, and everyone I talked to just shook their heads and felt like me, thinking my ex could not stoop any lower. This was beneath anything – he was hurting *his children*.

Did he not realize that he was hurting them, not me, or did he simply not care because he was more concerned about speeding up the divorce process and was throwing a temper tantrum?

I understand the laws and feel it is good that both parents have to sign the passport application for minor aged children.

It's probably not a huge problem for most, as they are likely dealing with normal parents; however, in my case, we had to deal with the childish behavior of an adult man.

It was not that I hadn't traveled with the kids on my own before, either. I had spent more vacations alone with my kids when we were married, than as a family with him traveling with us.

It was not like they did not have passports before, or that there was a danger of me taking the kids and fleeing the country.

There was simply no reason for him to act the way he did.

Yes, looking back, it is funny – maybe even hilarious – imagining this grown man stamping his feet like a toddler.

What did I learn from this experience? I feel that he destroyed the trust he had with our children. They trusted him up to this point, but feeling intentionally being targeted in this "war" hurt. It shifted us closer together, and they also learned that sometimes life takes us on a bit of a detour.

I learned that I truly needed to protect and embrace my children. I also learned that no matter how erratic my ex's behavior, the right way always wins.

Yes, I felt helpless, as there was nothing I could do to get the passports for my children. However, I also learned to trust my gut and the Universe, and rest assured that all would be well eventually, no matter what. Despite the fact that I felt my hands were tied, I learned to let go and trust that things would work out.

I also found out that I could not expect any real cooperation from Toni anymore. Even in matters concerning his own children, he put his desires before everything and everyone.

It was a valid lesson, and it was one of many turning points from feeling like cooperative parents (even though separated) to being a *single mom* fully and completely. Not only did I have to do everything on my own for their daily care, now I knew I would even have to fight with my ex for the rights of my children. It was no longer getting along for the sake of the children. It simply was him with his girlfriend against us (me and the children).

It was tough at first, as I always tried to see the good in every person and I could never fully understand the people out there who do not put the safety, health, and wellbeing of their own children first and foremost. I know he is not the only one, and I send love and hugs to all the single parents out there who have to take extra care of their children on their own.

What about the passports, you might wonder.

Well, a couple of weeks later, he grudgingly signed the forms in time for the kids to be able to participate in their trips. I guess his lawyer was able to talk some sense into him. Our children's passports had nothing to do with the divorce proceedings and this way of acting out was beneath even him.

Who knows? It does not matter. We were happy to be able to get new passports and for me, it was never about winning, it was about doing the right thing for our children.

They all have their passports now. The last time we needed to get them renewed, I was divorced and had sole custody of my children, so I did not need his signature any longer. Passport renewals are easy now. Once they are 18 and have reached their legal age of maturity, they won't even need a parent's signature any longer.

This was one of the funnier stories of going through a divorce, or at least one that I can laugh about now. It taught me a lot about myself: I am able to stand up for my children and I had a working inner compass for common sense.

Wisdom from within:

I do this exercise whenever I get stressed or face a situation in which I need to trust the Universe:

- I put my hands on my heart and start breathing into my hands.

This helps me calm down immediately and feel the trust.

You can also ask the Universe for support. Our helpers are eager to assist us anytime and with anything. Simply ask them for help, out loud or in your head. The more you work with them, the better you will get at understanding their responses.

♥

TWENTY PERCENT LESS

Does the saying, "when it rains, it pours," relate to you?

Oh dear, yes! It's a saying I could completely relate to. It often felt like it was pouring – really pouring down on me. Sometimes I felt like I was still being kicked even though I was down.

It was November 2011, about half a year after I moved into my new home with my kids and Toni had sold our old home. He was so happy to have found a buyer and so eager to make big bucks out of the sale. Up to that point, he was paying us child support each month.

Then in November, he sent a payment that was 20% less than normal, without any warning. I was really worried and so shocked. I remember that I collapsed on my bed and just cried and cried. I asked the Universe, "Why does he do this to me? What have I done to deserve this?" It really felt like it never rained, it only poured.

I was devastated, to say the least. I was able to pay off the school fees at a monthly rate and was just about finished paying off the debts from my move, but now he suddenly decreased my income by a fifth.

What would you do if your company all of a sudden just paid you 20% less, without a warning, without talking to you beforehand?

I sent him an email telling him that he had paid too little. He simply wrote back saying he couldn't afford to pay more at the moment.

I was so sad, and I felt like he treated me like shit. He didn't even have the decency to have a conversation about it! I mean, any decent human being would have come to me and shared that they might not have enough money to pay what was promised and we could have found a solution to it. His way, though, was just shorting me without at least telling me so that I could make arrangements with my creditors or even buy food that month. It was not OK at all, but this – I was discovering – was how he worked.

You see, money was the only stronghold he had over me. Money was the only power he still had in my life. Everything else, I managed very well without him and he was losing his grip.

Plus, I know he felt he was supposed to have big money coming from the house sale; however, he forgot that he owed most of it the bank. So, while he was able to sell the house, he did not get as much money as he'd anticipated, so it seemed he just shorted his ex-wife and kids, because he could.

I couldn't do anything about it. I couldn't talk to my lawyers. Toni never signed anything, so as long as he paid *something* he was OK by the law. And I couldn't try to explain to him that this left us in a pretty bad situation, financially. He didn't care about our needs. All he was thinking of was himself.

This was a bad situation for the kids and me because, with 20% less income, all I could afford was to pay my fixed costs: rent, school, lease of my car, and that was it. I had nothing to live off. Yes, I know I had a roof over my head and I still counted myself lucky, as I had three gorgeous children, too. Not knowing where I would get money for food or milk, let alone pay extra bills like sports or even gasoline for the car was really hard.

Toni kept paying me 20% less till our divorce was final in 2014, no matter what hardship we went through. He couldn't care less. By that time, he did not even see his kids anymore, so he had no extra costs like for food or vacations with them. Nothing. I had no break from responsibility either.

For us, it was a hard time, but I learned to stand up for myself even more. I remembered that, as a teenager, I had gone to the tax office to explain my cause, so I gathered all my strength and did so again. I called, emailed, and wrote to everyone who was sending me bills, explaining my situation. Most of them were very understanding and granted me a reprieve. Others told me they had nothing to do with it and I was due to pay immediately. During this time, I learned to stand up, speak up, and explain my situation, which was something I had not done in such a long while. It felt very awkward and weird at first, but the more I stood up, the more I was able to do so.

Yes, we survived I sold everything I could, just to make a bit of money and I am also grateful for friends and family who lent me money over that time. I knew I would receive some shares and options at the divorce, so I would be able to fully pay back my debts to each debtor and those who had lent me money.

We spent the most amazing summer at home, doing little day trips instead of spending money on vacation. I still have fond memories of it.

During this time, I also learned that the Universe always provides. I was reluctant to accept loans at first. I was so fixated on getting the money from Toni, as I felt he was obligated to make sure his three kids were well cared for. Only when I fully gave up, when it was clear Toni would not be the one to rescue us – never was, never would be – was I able to step back and allow others to step in.

When one door closes, don't keep knocking on that door. Step back and look for other doors. There is never only one door, especially not if it is closed.

I was able to receive and accept help. It felt great, as I always felt like I was so alone on my journey and I always felt like I needed to find a way to figure it all out myself. Thankfully, there were others who were ready to step in.

We all have helpers in every situation if we only let them assist us. It was with deep gratitude that I received assistance from friends and family and this has helped me to open my heart more. It became a path of survival instead of the battle of the divorce. It was now more the path *to* Caroline and less the path *against* Toni.

At the divorce hearing, it was agreed that he had to return to paying 100% of what we had originally agreed to, and this time I got it in writing.

Trust goes a long way; however, trusting an ex might not always be in one's own best interest.

Twenty percent less might sound great during a sale in a shop, but if it means twenty percent less income, it is not at all the same feeling.

Wisdom from within:

Fear is a daunting feeling. It sometimes feels like a fist is hitting your belly. Fear gets stuck in your solar plexus, which is situated below the breastbone, in between the lower ribs.

You can breathe into this area, allowing beautiful warm sunshine clear that area is very helpful.

Cutting cords on a regular basis is a must.

I love to cleanse away lower energy while taking a shower. I ask the Universe to rinse away all fear, worries, sorrows and pains.

Salt baths are also very useful to clear away lower energies and they also help us relax more.

♥

VANISHED CHRISTMAS PRESENTS

Was there a moment where you could only shake your head?

This story is actually funny, and no one got hurt. It is another laughable example of Toni's attempt to control us. It felt like a toddler's temper tantrum, a desperate grasp for control.

There was this one Christmas when all three kids did NOT want to go to their dad's for Christmas. I was fine with it. By then, I had already learned to listen to my children and not force them to do anything that did not feel right for them. I had done that, learned from it, and learned to trust my own instincts much more by then.

All my children have our (Toni and my) friends as godparents. We purposely did not choose siblings, as we felt they were already aunts and uncles and we wanted to widen the "family circle" a bit more.

Two of the three children's godfathers work in the city and, of course, they are all friends with both Toni and me.

Instead of coming all the way out to us, they chose to drop off the Christmas presents for the kids at Toni's office, so that he could pass the presents on to the kids for them.

It seemed like a good arrangement.

However, as I mentioned, this was the Christmas the kids chose NOT to go to their dad's house. They'd been there several Christmases before and had felt ignored and unhappy visiting.

So, when I got Toni's email telling us that the kids would only get their godfather's presents if they came to his home, I did not know whether I should laugh or cry. It felt like child's play and it felt like blackmail.

I did feel sorry for him. Did he truly feel he could force his kids to come to him or bribe them with the goodies of the presents they should have gotten anyway, as they were coming from their godfather?

I sat back and thought for a moment. I felt it was OK for him to only give them presents from *him* when they visited him. I understood and was fine with that.

However, it was not OK to withhold the presents from their godfather, presents that were handed to him in good faith and trust, presents that should have been forwarded on to the children.

What did I do then? Of course, I shared this news with my kids. I explained in, simple facts, and let them choose what they wanted to do.

None of them wanted to visit their father, not even with the extra bonus of presents, which was very understandable to me.

I realized that my kids had learned to be more assertive and that they had matured a lot, no matter their age. I was proud of them and also sad for them.

I always wished for a great and loving father for my kids. I knew they would come to know the father they had, rather than the father we wished they had. Getting to know him and accept him was a process. It took time.

When Toni and I were still together, as I mentioned before, I bridged the emotional gap between him and the kids; however, now that this bridge was no longer there, the kids learned to see their father as he was, not as he could have been. This was a natural learning process for them and, even though it was painful, it was also very wonderful to see that my kids could not be bought.

I could take a step back and let the situation unfold. Again, I learned that there was nothing I had to do, nothing I had to say. All I ever needed to do was hold out my arms to embrace my kids and be there for whenever they needed me.

I also learned that I no longer needed to protect my kids. They were strong enough to deal with their father just the way he was. They were ready, ready to get to know him on a new level: face-to-face.

What happened to the gifts? We don't know. They never found their way to us. The kids never got the presents from their godfathers that year. Of course, I wrote the godfathers and told them that, as Toni did not forward their presents, the kids had not received anything. I thanked them for their effort and understanding.

One of the godfathers started coming to us every Christmas and birthday after that incident. He is a wonderful friend to me and such an awesome godfather to Catherine. He is always happy to see the boys too. I am glad my children have a great male role model in their life in the form of this dear friend.

To this day, we smile about this story. I sometimes wonder how I would have acted were I in Toni's shoes. Very different, I suppose.

Wisdom from within:

Sometimes all we can do is breathe. I usually put my hands below my belly button and breathe into my hands – deep belly breaths all the way down. I concentrate on the breathing; this is calming, soothing and relaxing.

When we concentrate on our breath, we also come out of fear mode and back into our hearts. I love to do this exercise and whenever something stressful comes up, I go back to my breath. It keeps me sane.

It also helps to count, so count to six while breathing in and count to eight while breathing out, letting go, releasing.

As an alternative, you can count to seven while breathing in, hold your breath for the count of seven, breathe out count to seven and then hold your breath again to the count of seven. Do this for a round of seven. You will feel more balanced.

I hope this helps you, too.

♥

EPILOGUE

How are you doing nowadays?

The kids and I have come such a long way over the last nearly ten years, ever since Toni announced he was moving out. I can only fully grasp how far we have come now, after having written the stories that longed to come out the whole time. Writing these stories was a healing journey for me too; I was able to let go and heal on yet a new level again.

Looking back, I am so proud of my three children: what we mastered together, how resilient we were, and how all those stories brought us closer together as a family and further along on our journey.

We are moving again, moving into an apartment. The time has come. We no longer need a big house with a garden and all the work it brings. It is time to simplify and make our lives easier. We are looking forward to the move, no matter how much decluttering still lies ahead of us. It's time to release and heal some more. Time to emerge fresh and recharged again.

Mathew is studying at a university close by and still lives at home.

Catherine will be off studying abroad this summer. I know I will dearly miss my daughter, but I also know we will always be connected, no matter where we live. I'm happy for the technology that keeps us in touch with one another, too.

Horatio is starting high school, and, in four years, we will see where life takes him.

The kids and I got a cat the first summer after the separation and she has been such a great emotional support for all of us. We love animals and it was great to choose such a loving and intuitive companion.

We also got a dog two years ago and he is amazing! He's so playful and has connected with all of our hearts because of the fun he brings to our lives.

Our tortoises are all doing well, too; we got some babies years ago and have a bunch of them now. Observing them sitting silently, just watching is beautiful and calms us all down. They remind us to make time for resting or hibernating phases in all our lives.

We all grow stronger through all our experiences. Learning to see the good in whatever comes our way, embracing the lessons, and seeing the blessing in it is the best way to deal with it all. Knowing that some things are not meant to be and some things come to an end is a great lesson we all have to learn as well and part of all of our lives.

I learned to take just one step at a time. One step is all that is ever needed. This also serves as a reminder for me when I go into overwhelm from starting my decluttering and moving process.

The kids and I are in a happy space now. We know we can deal with most curve balls thrown at us. I am contentedly making my own choices and decisions now and, of course, always including my three children.

Naturally, Toni tried to renegotiate the divorce contract – to shorten our allowance – right when I started writing this book. Of course, I felt the fear and intimidation rise in me again; however, it took me only a moment to remember to breathe and come back into my heart, then I was ready to write a very clear message back. I have come a long way from that shy, dependent, *trying to please everyone* young woman I was ten years ago, indeed.

I hope that sharing my stories has inspired you and that, if you are facing a similar situation, you remember to take one step at a time and keep focusing on the light at the end of your tunnel. It does get better and easier as you keep going.

"We never know how strong we are, till being strong is the only option we have." (A gorgeous quote from Bob Marley)

I never realized what a people-pleaser I had become until the person I tried to please most removed himself from my life. What a relief it was and the amount of freedom the separation brought to me is something I can only fully grasp now.

Warm hugs to all the recovering doormats out there. You are not alone. Your time is now. Embrace the journey to learn how to do the things you love to do and learn to please yourself and put your own needs into the equation. It might be weird at first, but it is a journey that is well worth it. You are worth it.

Thank you for reading my stories. Thank you from the bottom of my heart for being part of my journey.

Warm hugs and much love,

Caroline

♥

A FINAL WISDOM FROM WITHIN:

I love to lie on the grass on my back. I feel how much I am carried by Mother Earth and all the stress can fall off of my shoulders as I simply lie there and breathe.

We often feel like we carry the burden of the world with us, probably on our shoulders. When we allow ourselves to lie down on the grass and just be, we can breathe in the realization that WE are carried and there is nothing we need to carry on our shoulders, everything is taken care of.

♥

ACKNOWLEDGMENT

I'd love to thank my three children for being part of this journey, for their patience and understanding, and for their love. Thank you for giving me the strength and purpose I needed plus all the cuddles, laughter, and joy along the way. Thank you for making this job, being Mom, so rewarding.

I am so very proud of you! Thank you for inspiring me and teaching me so many lessons, for the bond we all share, and for enriching my life by eons.

I love you with all of my heart.

Always,

Your Mom

I'd also love to thank all my friends and family that helped me through this time; I deeply appreciate you all.

SPECIAL THANKS GO TO

Susan Ellis-Saller, the most amazing Editor. Thank you so much for being such a wonderful friend and also for using your magic wand over my writing and beautifying it even more. I love how you work so in sync (intuitively) with what I want to express, finding an even better way of describing it. Thank you for being part of this book.

Sean Patrick, for being such an amazing Publisher and Book Coach. Thank you for seeing what my book was going to be, long before I even knew how to put it all together. Writing this book while you cheered me on made such a difference, as well as your positive insights. Thank you for all your expertise and for helping me make my dream of being a published author come true.

ABOUT THE AUTHOR

Caroline is a Heart Flow Healer who lives with her three teenage children and pets, including a dog, cat, and nine tortoises, surrounded by the healing nature of Switzerland.

Through her journey, she has learned how to rise up, look after herself and become more assertive whilst also helping others to open doors to love.

Caroline loves to inspire and spread love. Love is our true essence and holding everyone in love - allowing everyone to reconnect with their true essence - is one of her most important aims.

As an Earth Angel, Empath, Introvert, and sensitive person, she has come a long way from feeling left out, not fitting in, and not feeling like she belonged to accepting herself fully and allowing her own colors to shine, feeling at home and loved.

Caroline loves to write. She has written many blog posts around topics of self-love, healing, relationship healing, and grief, as well as previous books: My Life With An Indigo Child (E-book available on PalmyHealing.com) and her contributions to Diana Cooper's 777 *Angel Stories* and Alex Blackwell's *Letting Go*.

Visit her online and get in touch with her at

palmyhealing.com

Printed in Germany
by Amazon Distribution
GmbH, Leipzig